Collins

KS2
Science

Study Book

KS2
Science
Study Book

Jon Goulding and Jennifer Smith

Contents

Asking Scientific Questions and Planning Enquiries

- Ask relevant questions
- Plan and set up scientific enquiries
- Recognise and control variables, and ensure a fair test

Asking the Question

Most enquiries in science start with a question that is designed to help something be even better understood. Finding the answer is the aim of the enquiry.

For example, if a scientist already knows that germination of a seed is the start of most plant growth, this knowledge could lead to the following question:

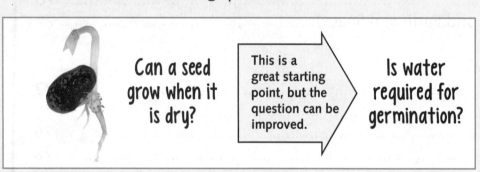

Can a seed grow when it is dry?

This is a great starting point, but the question can be improved.

Is water required for germination?

Careful thought is needed about exactly what the question is asking. The enquiry could investigate everything a seed might need in order to grow, but that would be a much larger task. It is also important to use correct vocabulary – plants *grow* but seeds *germinate*.

Planning a Scientific Enquiry

The next step is to plan how to investigate the question. This is known as the method of the enquiry – what will be done to try to find the answer to the question.

The equipment to be used will need thinking about, as well as how to measure the outcomes. For example, seeds, water and a dish to put them in will be needed, and the outcome could be measured by observing the seeds.

The seeds could be placed on cotton wool in a dish. Some cress seeds (which germinate relatively quickly) could be placed on wet cotton wool, and others on dry cotton wool.

Key Point

Questions are good starting points for an enquiry.

Tip

Be specific in questions and use scientific words.

Tip

Make sure you plan to use equipment that is readily available, and that you know how to use it.

Controlling Variables

When planning the method of enquiry, consideration must be given to the things that could affect the outcome. These are known as **variables**.

Could any of these play a part in the seed germination enquiry?

Temperature?   Amount of water?   Size of dish?   Type of seed?

Study

Tip

Always ask yourself, 'What is the aim of the enquiry?' This will help you to control the correct variables.

Creating a Fair Test

In a **fair test**, only the variable being tested is changed.

Example

To make sure that the seed germination is a fair test:

- each dish should be placed in the same location at the same time
- the dishes should be exactly the same size
- the type and amount of cotton wool should be the same
- the type and number of cress seeds should also be the same.

The only variable which changes is the presence of water. The cotton wool in one dish should be dry and in the other dish, wet.

Quick Test

1. What does a scientific enquiry begin with?
2. Which step in planning an enquiry deals with **how** it will be done?
3. What is meant by the term 'fair test'?

Key Words

- Method
- Variables
- Fair test

Collecting and Recording Data

- Make systematic and careful observations
- Take accurate measurements using appropriate equipment and methods
- Use standard units when recording data

Taking Measurements

Always consider exactly what should be measured. This will help in choosing the correct equipment and the correct unit of measure.

If measuring how much some plant shoots grow in a certain number of days following germination, a ruler is needed to measure in centimetres or millimetres. It is also useful to provide more information, for example how many seeds germinated.

If measuring the change in temperature of the contents of a beaker of snow when left in the classroom for a day, careful observation, a thermometer and a clock or watch will be required.

If measuring temperature change over time, for example, when testing the insulating properties of a material, a thermometer and stopwatch, or a data logger, are needed.

The correct units should be chosen and used when measuring, for example:

temperature: **°C**   length or distance: **mm, cm or m**

time: **seconds, minutes and hours**

Accuracy in observations and measurement should be ensured.

Key Point

Sometimes, measurement is not needed but careful observation is, for example, when looking for signs of germination in cress seeds.

Tip

Whatever measuring equipment you are using, it is vital that you read the scale carefully. Be accurate.

Observing and Recording Data

Once data has been collected, a little more thought is needed before any answer is given to the question posed by the enquiry.

Repetition helps check the reliability of data. To be more certain about data, the investigation should be repeated (more than once ideally) in case there were other factors affecting the investigation.

Recording of observations and measurements should be systematic and in a simple form. Using a table helps to keep data clear and organised.

This table shows how the temperature of the contents of a beaker, initially full of snow, changed over the course of a day in the classroom.

Time	9 am	10 am	11 am	12 pm	1 pm	2 pm	3 pm
Temp (°C)	–2.0	4.0	9.0	12.0	14.0	15.0	15.5

It was essential that the temperature was measured every hour.

Here is a table showing the amount of water that evaporated in 24 hours from beakers in different locations around the home.

Location	Bedroom	Airing cupboard	Fridge	Freezer	Kitchen
Amount (ml)	15	32	2	0	18

Careful measurements of the amount of water remaining in each beaker were taken at the end of the 24-hour period, allowing a calculation of how much water had evaporated.

> **Tip**
>
> Repeating an investigation with several samples will help to rule out other factors which could affect the data.

Quick Test

1. For the evaporation enquiry above, name two variables that must be kept the same.
2. Using the table above, in which location did most evaporation occur?
3. Why should an enquiry be repeated with several samples?

Key Words

- Reliability of data

Making Conclusions

- Present findings from enquiries
- Report on findings from enquiries
- Draw conclusions from data

Presenting Findings

Using tables to record data can help to:

- keep data organised
- spot patterns in the data.

Look at the first table on page 7. If the original question was *How does the temperature of the contents of a beaker, initially filled with snow, change during a day in the classroom?* then it can be seen that the temperature rises throughout the day. This can also be shown as a graph:

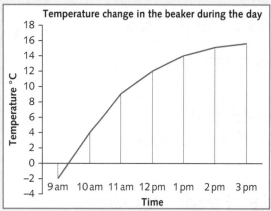

This line graph really helps to show the change in temperature over time.

From the second table on page 7, it is possible to work out where the water evaporated most, but this can be made more visual by use of a bar chart. If the original question was, *How does evaporation of water differ in different indoor locations?* it can be seen from the table, and more clearly from the bar chart, that more water evaporates in the airing cupboard than in the other locations.

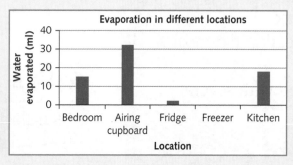

Reporting Findings and Drawing Conclusions

It is one thing to record and present data from an enquiry, but quite another to then draw useful conclusions.

A simple conclusion from the snow enquiry would be that the temperature of the snow rises in the classroom. This is true, but could have been guessed without going to the effort of putting the snow in a beaker and recording the temperature each hour. When looking at the data, the question of how the temperature changes needs to be answered.

Looking at the line on the graph, it can be seen that it starts quite steep before becoming less steep. This helps in drawing the simple conclusion that temperature rises as time passes. However, it also allows the conclusion that the temperature in the beaker rises quickly to begin with before slowing down.

Reporting all of this requires the data to be presented (using the line graph) alongside a written conclusion. The conclusion could simply state:

> The temperature in the beaker placed in the classroom rises at a decreasing speed as time passes. (This is just a more formal way of saying that the temperature rises more slowly as time goes on.)

Looking at the data from the evaporation enquiry, an assumption has to be made when drawing the conclusion – the freezer is clearly the coldest place in the house and, in most homes, an airing cupboard will be the warmest.

The simple conclusion for this enquiry is that:

> The warmer the location, the more evaporation occurs.

As with all scientific enquiries though, conclusions often lead to further questions, as can be seen in the next section.

Tip

When looking at your data, ask yourself, 'So what?' Think carefully about what the data shows you.

Quick Test

1. Why is a chart such as a graph or bar chart useful for presenting data?
2. How would you present data showing change over time?
3. What is the purpose of the conclusion to an enquiry?

Key Word

- Conclusion

Using Evidence and Improving Enquiries

- Use evidence to answer questions
- Identify evidence that has been used to support or refute ideas or arguments

Identifying and Using Evidence

The question asked earlier for the germination enquiry was: *Is water required for germination?* If the seeds with water germinated, and those without water did not, this can be used as evidence that water is required for the germination of cress seeds.

It is important to identify and refer to the evidence being used to answer the enquiry question. However, there also needs to be confidence in the evidence. The enquiry could be repeated, and evidence can be discussed in terms of the percentage of seeds germinating, and amount of water used. When answering the question, it is important to ask whether this evidence is good enough to be able to give a confident answer.

Tip

Always question your results – ask yourself whether everything done was as reliable and accurate as it could have been.

Improving the Enquiry

When looking at evidence also think of ways to improve the enquiry. Consider if anything could have been done differently, such as using different equipment or making the test more reliable. It may be that the enquiry is then repeated with any changes made. Evidence from an enquiry can also be used to lead to further questions and enquiries to deepen scientific knowledge. For example:

Does temperature play a part? Do all seeds behave in the same way? What are the best conditions for germination? Would soil make any difference?

Quick Test

1. Why is it important to be confident in the evidence used?
2. Why might an enquiry sometimes need to be done again?

Key Word

- Evidence

Practice Questions

Challenge 1

1   What equipment would you need to measure the temperature of water?

_____

1 mark

2   What is the 'method' of an enquiry?

_____

1 mark

3   Why might you record data in a table?

_____

1 mark

Challenge 2

1   You are asked to measure how quickly boiling water cools in different-shaped containers. What equipment would you need?

_____

_____

1 mark

2   How would you ensure this is a fair test?

_____

_____

_____

3 marks

Challenge 3

1   The table below shows the size of bean plants after being left to grow in different places for two weeks.

Plant location	Window sill	Dark cupboard
Growth (cm)	34	10

Assuming all variables were the same apart from the location, what can you conclude from this data?

_____

_____

2 marks

2   How could the reliability of the data above be improved?

_____

1 mark

Grouping Living Things

- Recognise that living things can be grouped in different ways
- Describe how living things are classified into groups
- Give reasons for classifying plants and animals based on specific characteristics
- Explore and use classification keys to help group, identify and name living things

Grouping Living Things in Different Ways

All living things can be put into one of three main groups:

- animals (key feature: cannot produce their own food)
- plants (key feature: produce their own food)
- micro-organisms (key feature: very small).

Animals can be grouped into:

- **vertebrates**, which have a backbone
- **invertebrates**, which have no backbone.

Vertebrates are then grouped as follows:

Group	Characteristics		Example
Mammals	• Have body hair (or fur) • Use lungs to breathe	• Babies born live, and drink milk • Body temperature steady	
Birds	• Have feathers • Use lungs to breathe	• Lay eggs • Body temperature steady	
Reptiles	• Have dry scales • Use lungs to breathe	• Lay eggs • Body temperature changes	
Amphibians	• Have damp skin • Use gills then lungs	• Lay soft eggs in water • Body temperature changes	
Fish	• Have scales • Use gills to breathe	• Lay soft eggs in water • Body temperature changes	

There are several groups of **invertebrates**. These include:

- worms
- snails and slugs
- spiders – 2 body parts, 8 legs
- insects – 3 body parts, 6 legs.

Scientists divide **plants** into two big groups. They are:

- **flowering plants**, including deciduous trees, grasses, shrubs, cereals
- **non-flowering plants**, such as coniferous trees, mosses, ferns and algae.

Tip

When classifying living things, always look for the most obvious clues first, such as: plant or animal; body covering (feathers, scales, damp skin, fur or hair); number of legs.

Using Classification

Classification of living things helps scientists understand different animals and plants. It also helps them to identify newly discovered and unknown species because they can make comparisons with the features of known species. Using the information on page 12 it is possible to find out where an animal belongs.

If it has scales, it could be a fish or a reptile. Taking a closer look might reveal that it has gills to breathe through. It is therefore most likely that it is a fish. If it has three body parts and six legs, it will be an insect.

Creating and Using a Key

A classification key can be created by asking questions about the key features being observed. Imagine an animal with scales. A very simple branched key for investigating what type of animal it could be might look something like this:

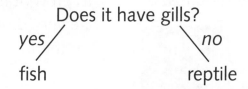

Does it have gills?

yes / \ no

fish   reptile

Quick Test

1. Using the information on page 12 to help you, complete the branched key below.

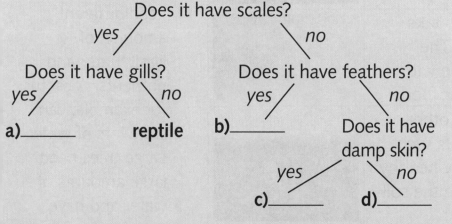

Does it have scales?

yes / \ no

Does it have gills?   Does it have feathers?

yes / \ no   yes / \ no

a)_____   **reptile**   b)_____   Does it have damp skin?

yes / \ no

c)_____   d)_____

2. What characteristics can help to distinguish between spiders and insects?
3. What is the main difference between a vertebrate and an invertebrate?

Parts of Plants

- Explore the requirements of plants for life and growth
- Describe the functions of different parts of flowering plants
- Explain how water is transported within plants

Requirements for Life and Growth

Before a seed can germinate it needs water, which usually comes from soil. Germination also requires food, which is contained within the seed.

During germination, most plants will start to grow a shoot and a root.

The shoot will grow (even through soil) towards a source of light and air.

The root will grow into the soil in search of water and nutrients.

Following germination, a healthy plant quickly requires:

Light: Plants need light to make food. The leaves of a plant use light, water and carbon dioxide from the air to make the food they need to grow.	
Water: Water is vital to life. Plants use water to help them make food. They take water in through their roots.	
Air: Plants use their leaves to take carbon dioxide from the air. The leaves use the carbon dioxide with water and light to make their food.	
Nutrients: Like humans and other animals, plants need nutrients such as minerals to help them stay healthy. They get these from water in the soil through their roots.	
Room: It is important for a plant to have room to grow. If it gets too crowded, a plant will find it difficult to get enough water and light.	

Key Point

All living things need water, food and air. Plants are like humans – if they don't have nutrients, they won't be as healthy. If they don't have space to grow, it makes life very difficult for them.

Key Point

Different plants need different amounts of light, water and nutrients. A cactus, for example, can store lots of water. Large trees need large amounts of water and have extensive roots.

Plant Part Functions

Flowers
Flowers are needed for reproduction. Colour and scent attract insects. Pollen and eggs are produced by the flowers and these are needed to produce seeds.

Leaves
Leaves are needed for nutrition because they make food for the plant using sunlight and carbon dioxide from the air in a special process called photosynthesis.

Stem
The stem is needed for support and for nutrition. It holds the plant up so it can get light, and it transports water and nutrients from the roots to the leaves and flowers.

In trees, the stem is known as the trunk.

Roots
Roots support the plant, acting as an anchor to prevent it blowing away. The roots are also vital for nutrition. Thousands of tiny root hairs absorb (soak up) water and minerals from the soil. The water and minerals then travel up through the plant.

Water Transport in Plants

Water absorbed by the roots travels up inside the stem of the plant. From the stem, the water can enter the leaves and flowers, helping the plant to grow and be healthy by delivering essential minerals to where they are needed.

Quick Test

1. List five things that a plant needs to grow healthily.
2. Which parts of a plant start to grow during germination?
3. Why are the leaves of a plant important?
4. What are the two main roles played by the stem of a plant?

Key Words

- Nutrients
- Germination

Life Cycles

- Describe the differences in the life cycles of a mammal, an amphibian, an insect and a bird
- Describe the changes as humans develop to old age

Life Cycles of Animals

The life cycle of an animal is the journey from the start of its life to the end of its life or to the point at which the animal has babies and new life is formed.

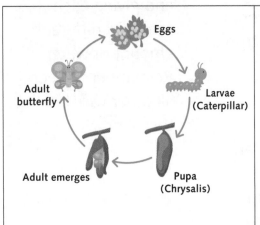

Insect life cycle

- Eggs are laid by the insect (e.g. a butterfly).
- Larva hatches from the eggs.
- Larva then becomes a pupa and changes into an adult insect.

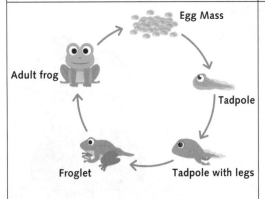

Amphibian life cycle

- Eggs are laid in water.
- Tadpoles begin to develop in the eggs.
- Tadpoles hatch and continue to grow in the water until they are adults.

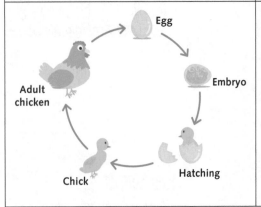

Bird life cycle

- Eggs are laid, usually in a nest.
- The baby bird develops in the egg before hatching.
- The chick continues to grow to adulthood.

Key Point

Remember that all living things eventually die; life cycles ensure new life replaces plants and animals that have died.

Working Scientifically

Observe (and use research as necessary) the differences and similarities of different animals at different stages of their life cycle.

Mammal Life Cycles

In the mammal life cycle, a fertilised egg develops into an embryo and then a foetus (a baby) inside the body of a female.

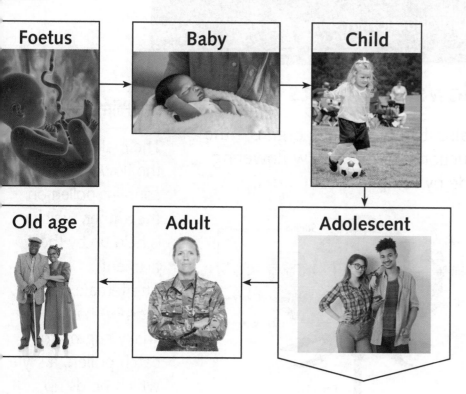

| Foetus → Baby → Child |
| Old age ← Adult ← Adolescent |

Puberty

During adolescence (approximately 10 to 18 years old), puberty causes the bodies of boys and girls to change.

Hairs start to grow on boys' bodies and faces, and their testicles start to produce sperm.

Girls develop breasts and wider hips and hair starts to grow on their bodies. Their ovaries begin to release an egg once every month. This is known as a period.

Quick Test

1. What is the name of the process during which the bodies of adolescent boys and girls change?
2. What is the difference between the way mammals reproduce and the way birds, reptiles and fish reproduce?
3. What is the common name given to the larvae of a butterfly?

Key Words

- Life cycle
- Puberty

Reproduction

- Explore the part that flowers play in the life cycle of flowering plants
- Describe the process of reproduction in some plants and animals

Reproduction in Flowering Plants

The flower of a plant contains its reproductive organs – the parts it uses during reproduction – to make new flowering plants. New plants are made by **sexual reproduction**.

Pollination

A flower's colourful petals and the scent of sweet nectar attract insects such as bees, which feed on the nectar.

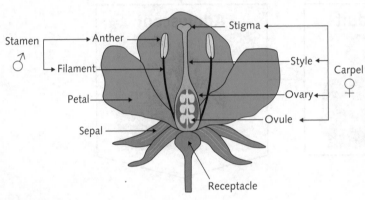

Pollen from the flower's anther sticks to the insect and is then carried to another flower where it sticks to the stigma. This process is called **pollination**.

Fertilisation

When a grain of pollen joins with an **egg** in the carpel of another flower, **fertilisation** takes place and a seed starts to form in the **ovary**.

Seed Dispersal

When a seed forms, the petals of the flower die and the ovary becomes a fruit containing the seeds. Some fruits are easily recognisable (such as fruits we eat) but for some plants, such as garden flowers, the fruit does not look like edible fruit at all. The fruit of the plant is important for seed dispersal. This is when the seeds are carried away from the parent plant (by animals, wind, exploding pods or water) to give them room to grow into new plants.

Key Point

The male part of the flower (**stamen**) contains pollen on the anther, which is held up by the filament.
The female part (**carpel**) has a sticky stigma to catch pollen, a style which holds up the stigma, and an ovary containing ovules.

Working Scientifically

Take cuttings from different plants and put them in soil. Do any of them start to grow? Consider the conditions and variables – temperature, amount of soil, amount of light and amount of water.

here are three common methods of seed dispersal:

Animal dispersal		Wind dispersal	Explosion dispersal

Some fruits stick to animals and the seeds are carried away.	Animals and birds eat some fruits, such as berries, and excrete them in a new place.	Light, feathery fruits help seeds be blown away by the wind.	Some fruits are pods which dry and then burst open, scattering the seeds.

Asexual Reproduction in Plants

ome plants can reproduce without pollen or an egg. This known as asexual reproduction. Small pieces cut from a lant (known as cuttings) can grow in the right conditions usually requiring at least water and light).

Reproduction in Animals

exual reproduction occurs in most animals. In this process:

the egg from the mother plus the sperm from the father combine and the egg is fertilised.

the fertilised egg grows into a foetus and eventually a baby is born.

his process is common to most animals, although in some, he embryo grows in an egg outside the mother. In humans nd other mammals, the baby grows inside the mother.

Quick Test

Complete the diagram.

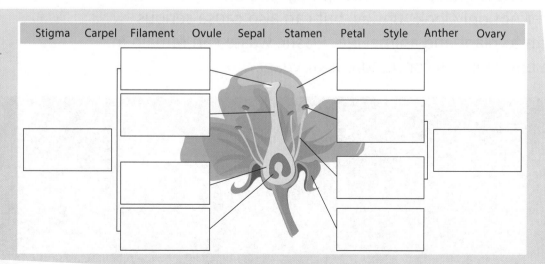

Stigma   Carpel   Filament   Ovule   Sepal   Stamen   Petal   Style   Anther   Ovary

Changing Environments

• Recognise that environments can change and that this can sometimes pose dangers to living things

Natural Changes

The environment, and specific **habitats**, change naturally over time, particularly as seasons change.

For example, a lake, river or pond will have different plants in and around it at different times of the year. These will attract different insects, birds and other animals, depending on the season.

Change in climate over longer periods of time can also cause environmental change.

Human Impact

Not all change is natural. Human activity can also cause environmental change. For example:

• building of homes, factories and roads
• chopping down trees to make space for farmland or building.

Such activity can destroy habitats and lead to deforestation, often leaving animals and plants without shelter or food. As the human population has increased, more damage has been done. Pollution is another major problem because it can poison animals and have a long-term effect on air and water quality and on the climate. Litter not only looks untidy, but can also cause serious harm to plant and animal life. Plastic waste can remain in the environment for hundreds of years.

Key Point

Pollution occurs when something that should not be there enters the environment or a habitat. This can include smoke from factory chimneys, sewage entering rivers and chemicals dumped in rivers or oceans or put on land to help crops grow.

Protecting the Environment

There are many ways in which humans can help protect the environment, including:

- recycling, which changes waste materials into new products
- reusing plastics, which reduces the amount of plastic waste entering the environment
- reducing the amount of plastic and other materials used in packaging products

creating a suitable habitat for animals and plants, which can help to protect them

supporting nature reserves, which help to protect habitats, and educate people about the need to look after them

creating a garden pond, which provides a small nature reserve in a garden and gives pond animals a safe place to live and reproduce

growing plants, which can attract more insects and birds to an area

creating environmentally friendly housing, which can reduce the impact of building work on habitats

using renewable energy sources such as wind power and solar energy (using energy from the sun), which can reduce pollution

planting trees, which can help offset the effects of deforestation and pollution.

Working Scientifically

Conduct a survey of the wildlife (plants and animals) you can see in two different locations (e.g. your garden or a local park and a town centre).

What are the differences?

What causes these differences?

Quick Test

1. Give two examples of human activity that damages the environment.
2. How can environmental damage impact animal and plant habitats?
3. Give two examples of how habitat creation can help plant and animal life.

Key Word

- Habitats

Practice Questions

Challenge 1

1 An animal with a backbone is called a _____ and
an animal without a backbone is called an _____.

2 marks

2 Explain a simple way to distinguish between an insect and a spider.

_____

_____

1 mark

3 Which part of a plant absorbs water from the soil?

_____

1 mark

Challenge 2

1 Write these stages of human life in order from youngest to oldest.

old age   adult   embryo   adolescent   child

_____   _____   _____   _____   _____

1 mark

2 In pollination, pollen from the _____ sticks to
the _____.

2 marks

3 Why are minerals important to a plant?

_____

_____

1 mark

Challenge 3

1 Name a common feature in the life cycle of an insect, bird, reptile and
amphibian that does not occur in humans.

_____

_____

1 mark

2 Explain the role of the leaves of a plant.

_____

_____

1 mark

3 Give **two** different ways in which the seeds of a plant can be dispersed.

_____

_____

2 marks

Review Questions

1   What is the purpose of a scientific enquiry?

_____

1 mark

2   If an enquiry is trying to find the best temperature for germination of seeds, what variable must be changed?

_____

1 mark

3   Explain your answer to question 2.

_____

_____

1 mark

4   What unit of measure would you use for the above enquiry?

_____

1 mark

5   An enquiry to find which surface has the least friction (which surface allows a ball to roll the furthest) tests four different surfaces, with a different size of ball used for each. Explain whether this is a fair test.

_____

_____

1 mark

6   Why should a scientific enquiry be repeated?

_____

1 mark

7   Look at the graph below.

Temperature change in the shed during the day

a) By how much did the temperature in the shed rise during the first hour?

_____

1 mark

b) The rate of warming was slower after 12 pm than before. How can you tell this from the line on the graph?

_____

1 mark

Food Chains

- Recognise that animals, including humans, need nutrition and cannot make their own food
- Identify producers and consumers; predators and prey
- Understand and interpret food chains

Producers and Consumers

Unlike plants, which are producers (make their own food), animals get all their nutrition by eating plants or other animals. All animals are consumers because they have to eat (consume) other living things. It is important that animals eat enough of the right foods to stay healthy.

A Food Chain

When one living thing eats another, a food chain begins.

Almost all food chains begin with a green plant (a producer) and finish with animals (consumers).

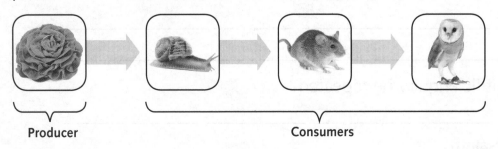

Producer   Consumers

Humans are Consumers

Humans need to consume a variety of different foods to get all the nutrients they need to stay healthy. They are part of many food chains because they are omnivores (eat both plants and animals).

Food Webs

Most animals need to eat more than one type of food. Food webs help to show how producers and consumers are linked and which animals eat the same foods.

Key Point

Consumers consume (eat) their food and producers produce (make) their food.

Key Point

A very small number of food chains start with micro-organisms, which produce nutrition through chemical reactions.

Tip

Remember that the arrows in a food chain show what each plant or animal is eaten by, not what something eats.

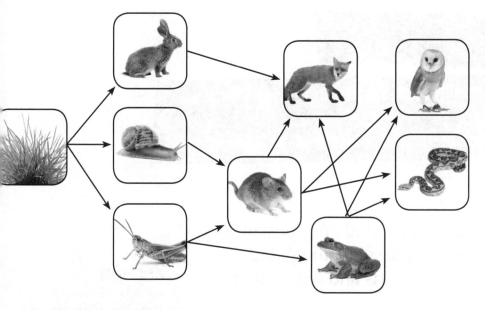

Predators and Prey

Animals that kill and eat other animals are called **predators** and the animals they eat are called **prey**.

Example

Some animals are both predators and prey in the same food web.

Prey   Predator

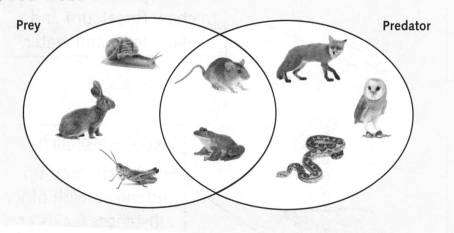

Working Scientifically

Food webs help to show relationships between plants and animals in the same habitat. Can you draw a food web that includes you? Think about the foods you eat and what other living things might be connected.

Key Point

Most animals eat more than one type of food and some can be both predators and prey.

Key Words

- Producers
- Consumers
- Food chain
- Omnivores
- Food webs
- Predators
- Prey

Quick Test

1. What is a plant known as in a food chain?
2. What do the arrows in a food chain/web show?
3. Complete the sentence: An animal that kills and eats another animal is called a _____.
4. Why do animals need to eat other living things?

Digestion

- Identify the parts of the digestive system in humans and describe their functions
- Identify different types of teeth and their functions in humans

Digestion

Digestion is all about breaking down food into substances the body can use. To do this, food passes through the **digestive system**, a series of body parts and organs that have different roles.

> **Key Point**
>
> Breaking down food = Digestion

The Digestive System

The digestive system provides the body with the nutrients and water it needs to function, grow, repair itself and stay healthy.

Step 1 – Mouth

Food and water enter the body through the mouth, which contains the tongue and the teeth.

Step 2 – Tongue and Teeth

The tongue and teeth help to chew (break up) and swallow food and water.

Step 3 – Oesophagus

Swallowed food is transported down a pipe called the **oesophagus** and into the **stomach**.

Step 4 – Stomach

Food is churned up and mixed with other substances (acids and enzymes) to help break it down even more.

Step 5 – Small Intestine

Food continues to be broken down into **nutrients** which are small enough to be **absorbed** (taken into) into the bloodstream and used by the body.

Step 6 – Large Intestine

Water is absorbed into the body, and undigested food is eliminated.

Teeth

The teeth are an important part of the digestive system. They crush, tear and slice up food, breaking it into smaller pieces which can be digested more easily. Humans have four different types of teeth: canines, incisors, molars and premolars.

Tooth	Appearance	Function (job)
Canines		Tearing and ripping tough food like meat
Incisors		Cutting and slicing food like fruits and vegetables
Molars		Grinding and crushing all types of food
Premolars		Grinding and crushing all types of food

Humans need all these different types of teeth to chew and break up a wide range of foods.

Humans will develop two sets of teeth over a lifetime. The 20 milk (baby) teeth are replaced by around 32 permanent (adult) teeth. This starts to happen around the age of 5.

Quick Test

1. What is the process of breaking down food called?
2. Which organ is responsible for the absorption of nutrients?
3. How many types of teeth do humans have?
4. What is the function of the incisors?
5. How many teeth does an adult have?

Key Point

Humans do not develop premolars until their permanent (adult) teeth erupt.

Working Scientifically

Look at some images of different animals' teeth. How are they different from yours? Why do you think this is?

Key Words

- Digestive system
- Oesophagus
- Stomach
- Intestine
- Absorbed
- Canines
- Incisors
- Molars
- Premolars

Skeleton and Muscles

- Know that humans and some other animals have skeletons and muscles
- Understand that the skeleton and muscles provide the body with movement, protection and support

The Skeleton

Humans, and lots of other animals, have a structure of bones inside them called a **skeleton**.

The skeleton has three main jobs:

1. supporting the rest of the body and keeping things in place
2. protecting important organs
3. helping with movement.

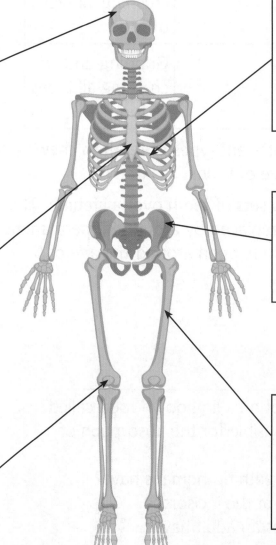

Skull (Cranium)

The main job of the **skull** is to protect the brain.

Ribs

The **ribs** form a ribcage which protects organs such as the heart and lungs.

Spine (Vertebrae)

The **spine** provides support and protects the spinal cord.

Pelvis

The **pelvis** supports the upper body and protects pelvic organs.

Kneecap (Patella)

The **kneecap** supports the movement of the legs and protects the joint.

Thigh Bone (Femur)

The **thigh bone** supports the weight of the upper body and aids movement.

The skeleton is not one solid piece. At the joints, the bones are held together by ligaments which, along with the muscles, enable the body to bend and move.

Muscles

Muscles help the body to move by providing the forces (pushes and pulls) needed to move the bones at the joints.

Muscles are attached to the bones by tendons. They work in pairs by pulling on the bones to make them move. When one muscle in a pair contracts (pulls), it gets shorter, and the other muscle relaxes (gets longer). The main muscles in the arm are the biceps and the triceps.

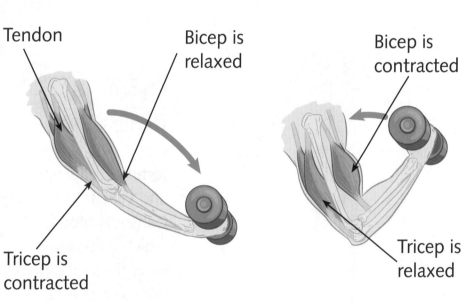

Tendon

Bicep is relaxed

Tricep is contracted

Bicep is contracted

Tricep is relaxed

Working Scientifically

Pick up a bottle of water in one hand and hold your muscles with your other hand. Feel the muscles as you lift and lower the bottle. Can you feel them contract and relax?

Quick Test

1. Complete the sentence: The combination of bones inside a human is called a _____.
2. What is the main job of the rib bones?
3. Other than protecting the organs, name one other job of the skeleton.
4. True or false? Muscles work in pairs.
5. Complete the sentence: When one muscle contracts the other _____.

Key Words

- Skeleton
- Skull
- Ribs
- Spine
- Pelvis
- Kneecap
- Thigh bone
- Ligaments
- Muscles
- Tendons

Heart and Blood Vessels

- Identify the main parts of the human circulatory system
- Describe how nutrients and water are transported within animals including humans

The Circulatory System

The **circulatory system** transports things like **oxygen**, nutrients and water around the body and helps eliminate (get rid of) waste like **carbon dioxide**.

It is made up of three main parts:

1. **blood**
2. **blood vessels**
3. **heart**.

Blood and Blood Vessels

Blood carries important materials around the body and keeps it healthy by protecting it against disease and infection. Blood is transported around the body in blood vessels.

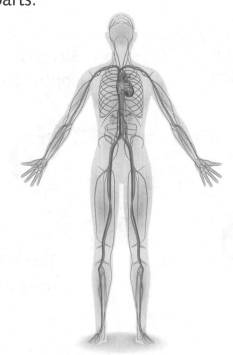

There are three different kinds of blood vessel:

- **Arteries**: transport **oxygenated** blood, containing nutrients and water from the heart to the body. They also transport blood from the heart to the lungs to collect oxygen.
- **Capillaries**: tiny blood vessels which allow substances like oxygen, carbon dioxide, water and nutrients to move into and out of the bloodstream.
- **Veins**: transport **deoxygenated** blood, carbon dioxide and other waste from the body back to the heart.

Key Point

The three main blood vessels (arteries, capillaries and veins) transport blood, which contains essential substances like oxygen and nutrients, around the body.

The Heart

The heart is a muscular organ that pumps blood around the body. It is located in the chest between the lungs and is connected to the blood vessels.

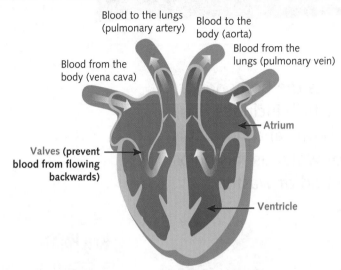

Blood to the lungs (pulmonary artery)

Blood to the body (aorta)

Blood from the lungs (pulmonary vein)

Blood from the body (vena cava)

Atrium

Valves (prevent blood from flowing backwards)

Ventricle

The muscles of the heart contract (tighten) and pump blood through arteries to the lungs to collect oxygen and remove carbon dioxide.

Oxygenated blood is transported back to the heart where it is pumped through the arteries, to the body, delivering oxygen and nutrients.

Deoxygenated blood that has been around the body and is carrying waste is transported back to the heart through the veins.

Muscles need more nutrients and oxygen when they are active, and they also produce more waste (carbon dioxide) which needs to be eliminated. So, when the body is active or exercising, the heart beats faster.

Study

Tip

You can check your heart rate (how fast the heart is beating) by checking your pulse. It is possible to find your pulse on your wrist and your neck. You can count how many times the heart beats in a minute.

Key Words

- Circulatory system
- Oxygen
- Carbon dioxide
- Blood
- Blood vessels
- Heart
- Arteries
- Oxygenated
- Capillaries
- Veins
- Deoxygenated
- Lungs
- Atrium
- Valves
- Ventricle
- Pulse

Quick Test

1. What is the job of the circulatory system?
2. Complete the sentence: The circulatory system is made up of blood, blood vessels and the _____.
3. Which blood vessels allow oxygen and nutrients to pass into the bloodstream?
4. True or false? Oxygenated blood is transported in veins.
5. Where is the heart located?

Healthy Living

- Recognise the impact of diet, exercise, drugs and lifestyle on how the body functions

A Healthy Diet

To stay healthy and get all the nutrients the body needs, humans need to eat a balanced diet which includes **fats**, **protein**, **carbohydrates**, **vitamins/minerals** and **fibre**. It is also very important to drink plenty of water as this helps the body to use the nutrients and get rid of waste.

Fats and oils provide energy, e.g. milk, butter, cheese, avocado

Carbohydrates provide energy, e.g. bread, pasta, potatoes, cereals, rice

Protein enables growth and repair, e.g. meat, eggs, fish, lentils, beans

Vitamins and minerals keep cells healthy, e.g. fruits and vegetables

Fibre keeps the digestive system moving, e.g. wholegrains, berries, sweetcorn, broccoli, nuts and seeds

Some types of fats, like unsaturated fats, are better for the body than others. Eating too much saturated fat and processed sugar (a form of carbohydrate) can be damaging to the body so should be eaten in moderation.

Keeping Active

Exercise and being active has many health benefits, including:

- keeping the heart and lungs strong and healthy
- improving fitness and muscle strength
- developing co-ordination
- preventing the body from storing too much energy as fat.

Key Point

Having a healthy diet is all about balance. Eating a variety of foods will make sure the body has all the nutrients it needs.

Key Point

Exercise and being active can also help you to feel happier and more confident and can be an excellent way of meeting new friends.

xercise uses the energy provided by food. If energy from ood is not used, it is stored in the body as fat. Storing too uch fat can lead to condition known as besity, which can cause any health problems cluding high blood ressure, diabetes and eart disease.

There are lots of fun ways to stay active.

voiding Damage

ome activities like drinking alcohol, smoking and using rugs can be bad for the body.

Activity	Damage to the body
Smoking	Bad for the heart and lungs and can cause heart attacks, cancer, blocked arteries and breathing problems. (Cigarettes contain a drug called nicotine which is highly addictive.)
Drinking alcohol	Bad for the liver, heart and stomach. It can affect memory and also increase blood pressure.
Taking drugs	Drugs can be very addictive and dangerous. They can damage the body in many different ways including causing damage to the brain.

Working Scientifically

When humans are active their hearts beat faster. Try checking your pulse when you are sitting down. Set a timer for a minute and see how many times your heart beats. Then try the same thing after doing some exercise. What do you notice?

Quick Test

1. What do foods like bread, pasta and potatoes provide for the body?
2. Complete the sentence: Eating a variety of foods, in the right amounts, is known as a _____.
3. Other than eating the right foods, what else can humans do to stay healthy?
4. Name an activity that can damage the body.

Key Words

- Fats
- Protein
- Carbohydrates
- Vitamins
- Minerals
- Fibre
- Drugs

33

Practice Questions

Challenge 1

1   Circle the correct underlined words to complete the sentence.

In a food chain, plants are known as <u>producers/consumers</u> and animals are known as <u>producers/consumers</u>.

2 marks

2   What are the organs responsible for breaking down food known as? Circle **one**.

the circulatory system   the digestive system   the skeleton

1 mark

3   Match the parts of the body to their functions.

Skeleton   Pumps blood around the body

Muscles   Supports the body and protects organs

Heart   Work in pairs to help the body move

3 marks

Challenge 2

1   In the food chain below, label the predator and the prey.

Grass   ➡   Rabbit   ➡   Fox

_____   _____   _____

2 marks

2   In the digestive system, what is the role of the stomach?

_____

1 mark

3   Which **two** types of teeth are responsible for crushing and grinding up food?

_____

2 marks

Challenge 3

1   Describe how humans can keep their bodies healthy. Include at least **two** things they should do and one thing they should avoid.

_____

_____

_____

3 marks

Review Questions

1   Why is the flower of a flowering plant usually brightly coloured?

    _____
    1 mark

2   How do plants get water to their leaves?

    _____

    _____
    1 mark

3   Why do plants need light?

    _____
    1 mark

4   What **two** things join together during fertilisation in a plant?

    _____   _____
    2 marks

5   Name **two** vertebrates and two invertebrates.

    Vertebrates: _____   _____

    Invertebrates: _____   _____
    4 marks

6   In an insect life cycle, what does the larva change into?

    _____
    1 mark

7   How does the birth of a bird differ from the birth of a mammal?

    _____
    1 mark

8   Complete the sentence: In sexual reproduction, an _____ from
    the woman is fertilised by a _____ from the man.
    2 marks

9   Give **two** examples of pollution.

    _____   _____
    2 marks

10 How can a nature reserve benefit plants and animals?

    _____

    _____
    2 marks

Adaptation and Variation

- Recognise that living things produce offspring of the same kind which are not identical to their parents
- Identify how plants and animals are adapted to their environments and understand that adaptations can lead to variations

Similarities and Variations

All living things produce offspring (young). Most of the time, children look like their biological parents because they inherit physical characteristics such as height, hair colour and eye colour.

While children might look similar to their parents, they are not identical. Each child will inherit and develop different characteristics. Although siblings (brothers and sisters) might look alike, they are all slightly different (except for identical twins). This is called variation.

Variations are the differences between plants and animals of the same species. They come from adaptations.

Adaptations

Adaptations are special characteristics which help a plant or animal to survive in a specific environment. They can either be inherited from parents or come from mutations.

Key Point

Children are similar to their parents but not identical; this is called variation.

Working Scientifically

Look at the litter of puppies (left). The puppies all have the same parents, but each puppy is slightly different. Make a list of the similarities and differences between the puppies. Can you predict what different characteristics the parents might have had?

Examples of Adaptations in Animals

Polar bear:

Webbed feet for swimming and walking on snow
Thick layer of fat for insulation and warmth
Special transparent fur for camouflage
Black skin to absorb heat from the Sun.

Camel:

- Thick coat of hair for camouflage and protection from the Sun
- Wide soft feet for walking on hot sand
- Hump of fat to store food and water
- Long thick eyelashes to protect eyes from sand.

Humans can adapt to almost any environment by building the right kinds of homes and wearing the right clothes.

Examples of Adaptations in Plants

Cacti live in hot environments with little water. Their adaptations include long roots to find water; waxy skin to help retain water; and small, needle-like leaves to help reduce water loss.

Waterlilies have adapted to living in water by having large flat leaves, long flexible stems and bowl-shaped flowers.

Key Point

Not all changes and adaptations are beneficial. When living things develop characteristics that are unhelpful, they are unlikely to survive and reproduce.

Key Point

Most plants and animals have adapted. Adaptations can help living things to survive in different environments.

Quick Test

1. True or false? Most offspring will look like their parents.
2. Name a characteristic that might be inherited.
3. What are the differences in the characteristics of plants and animals of the same species known as?
4. What is it called when a plant or animal has changed to suit its environment?

Key Words

- Offspring
- Inherit
- Characteristics
- Variation
- Adaptations
- Environment
- Mutations

Evidence for Evolution

- Recognise that living things have changed over time and that fossils provide information about what lived on Earth millions of years ago

Evolution

Evolution is the theory of how living things have adapted and changed over long periods of time or over many generations.

Plants and animals alive today are not the same as they were millions of years ago – they have made lots of small changes and adaptations.

The way something evolves depends on its environment and what it needs to do to survive. Different animals can evolve from the same ancestor, adapting different characteristics over many generations to suit different environments.

Key Point

Even humans have evolved over millions of years.

How Evolution Happens

1. Living things with useful adaptations survive and reproduce.
2. Offspring inherit these adaptations and develop some of their own through mutation.
3. This process continues and, over many generations, adaptations become more focused to the needs of the environment.

Natural selection plays an important role in evolution. The peppered moth is a good example of this.

1. At first, peppered moths were mostly a pale, whitish colour.
2. Pollution from factories made tree trunks darker which meant birds could see the paler moths on the trees.
3. The birds ate the paler moths.
4. The darker moths were camouflaged and survived, producing offspring with the same darker colour.

Key Point

Evolution is the theory of how living things have changed and adapted over long periods of time or many generations.

On the lighter bark, the paler moth can barely be seen. It is camouflaged.

Against the darker bark, the paler moth can easily be seen.

Only the darker moths that were able to camouflage survived to pass on these characteristics, so most new peppered moths were a darker colour.

Fossils

Fossils are the remains or impressions of plants or animals imprinted in rocks. They can be compared to things that are alive now to show how living things have changed over millions of years.

Prehistoric lizard skeleton

Fossil ferns

It is possible to tell when a fossil was formed and how old it is from the layer of rock that it is found in. Deeper layers of rock contain older fossils.

Scientists can date fossils and put them in order to see the small changes that have happened to a plant or animal over time. This provides evidence for the theory of evolution.

Quick Test

1. What is the name of the theory of how living things have changed over time?
2. Complete the sentence: When a living thing has changed over time, we say it has _____.
3. What can scientists study to compare living things with plants and animals from millions of years ago?

Key Point

Evolution happens because environments are always changing and living things face different challenges in order to survive.

Working Scientifically

These are fossils of plants and animals (left) that lived long ago. Can you see any differences or similarities to plants and animals that are alive today?

Key Words

- Evolution
- Generations
- Ancestor
- Natural selection
- Fossils

Practice Questions

Challenge 1

1 Use the words provided to complete the sentence.

> offspring   inherit

Most _____ look like their parents because they _____ some of their physical characteristics.

`2 marks`

2 Match these plants and animals to their adaptations.

Cactus   Webbed feet for swimming

Duck   Needle-like leaves to prevent water loss

Bat   Large ears to help navigate in the dark

`3 marks`

3 True or false? Evolution happens because living things adapt and change to suit their environment. _____

`1 mark`

Challenge 2

1 What characteristics might you inherit from your parents? Name **two**.

_____   _____

`2 marks`

2 Polar bears are highly adapted to their environment.

WS

a) What might happen if a polar bear wasn't adapted to its environment?

_____

`1 mark`

b) Name **two** ways that the polar bear has adapted.

_____

`2 marks`

3 How do fossils help scientists see how living things have evolved?

_____

_____

`2 marks`

Challenge 3

1 Giraffes have extremely long necks and eat leaves from very tall trees. Describe how and why giraffes might have developed such a long neck. Use your knowledge of adaptations and evolution to help you.

_____

_____

_____

`4 marks`

Review Questions

1 In a food web, is a caterpillar a producer or a consumer? _____

1 mark

2 True or false? An animal can be both a predator and prey. _____

1 mark

3 Tick the organs and body parts that are a part of the digestive system.

Tongue and teeth   Oesophagus   Heart

Muscles   Small intestine   Brain

3 marks

4 Circle the correct underlined word to complete the sentence.

The canine/incisor teeth are responsible for tearing and ripping food.

1 mark

5 How many sets of teeth do humans have in a lifetime? _____

1 mark

6 Name the **three** main parts of the circulatory system.

_____

_____

3 marks

7 Match the blood vessels to their function.

Capillaries   Transport blood containing oxygen from the heart to
                the body.

Arteries   Allow oxygen and nutrients to pass from the blood to
                the body.

Veins   Transport blood containing carbon dioxide to the heart.

3 marks

8 Sunflower oil, cheese and butter all provide the body with the
   same nutrient.

   a) Which type of food are they? _____

1 mark

   b) What do they provide the body with? _____

1 mark

9 Name **two** benefits of exercise on the body.

_____

_____

2 marks

10 Name **two** things that can damage the body.

_____

_____

2 marks

Solids, Liquids and Gases

- Compare and group materials as solid, liquid or gas
- Observe changes of state and measure or research temperatures at which they happen

Three Groups for all Materials

All materials fall into one of three groups known as states of matter. Each group has different properties.

Solids

- A solid holds its shape, and its volume without support.
- The shape of a solid does not change unless it is broken, cut or squashed into a different shape.

Liquids

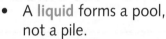

- A liquid forms a pool, not a pile.
- Liquids flow downwards.
- A liquid takes the shape of the container it is in. Its volume stays the same if it is moved into a larger container.

Gases

- A gas changes shape according to the container it is in.
- The volume of a gas expands to fill larger containers or can be compressed to fill smaller containers.
- Most gases are invisible.

Changes of State

Some materials change from one state to another when they are heated or cooled. The main processes for this are condensation, freezing, melting and evaporation.

Condensation

When gases are cooled, they turn into liquid.

Warm air (gas) inside a building or car cools (condenses) into water droplets (liquid) on the cool glass of a window.

Freezing

When liquids are cooled enough, they freeze and turn into a solid.

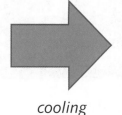

When water (liquid) is placed in a freezer, it cools and becomes ice (a solid).

cooling

cooling

heating

Evaporation

When a liquid is heated, it turns into a gas.

Heat from the Sun dries puddles because the liquid water evaporates into a gas (water vapour).

heating

Melting

When solids are heated, they can turn into liquid.

When a solid such as an ice lolly (mostly water) is heated, it melts.

Key Point

Different materials change state at different temperatures. Most metals are solid at room temperature, although mercury is liquid. Water is liquid at room temperature. It freezes at 0°C.

Gas condenses into liquid when it is cooled. Liquid freezes into a solid when it is cooled. A solid melts into liquid when heated. Liquid evaporates to gas when it is heated. Water freezes at 0°C, becoming a solid (ice). It boils at 100°C, the temperature at which water evaporates most rapidly. Iron remains solid until it reaches its melting point of 1536°C.

Quick Test

1. At what temperature does water change from liquid to solid?
2. What is the process known as when a liquid turns into a gas?
3. Write the name of one material in each box below.

Solid	Liquid	Gas

Key Words

- Solid
- Liquid
- Gas
- Condensation
- Freezing
- Melting
- Evaporation

43

The Water Cycle

- Identify the role played by evaporation and condensation in the water cycle
- Associate the rate of evaporation with temperature

The processes of evaporation and condensation play an important role in the Earth's weather patterns and in the water cycle that is so important for life on Earth.

Evaporation

Oceans, lakes, rivers and other bodies of water are essential to the weather on Earth. Evaporation plays a major role. As the Sun heats the surface of bodies of water, the water from the surface becomes a gas (water vapour) and rises into the sky.

Condensation

As the water vapour rises, it starts to cool and condense, forming clouds. Clouds consist of millions of droplets of water.

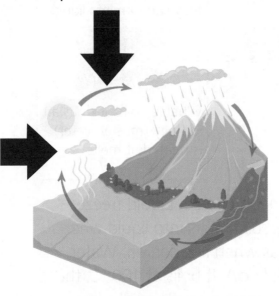

Key Point

Water on Earth is in a cycle and much of it changes state between liquid and gas during the water cycle.

When the water droplets in the clouds become too big and heavy for the air to hold them, they fall as **precipitation** (which takes many forms, including rain, snow and hail) and finds its way back into rivers, lakes and oceans. This cycle is continuous – water is constantly going round in the water cycle.

Without evaporation and condensation, this process could not happen.

Evaporation and Temperature

Evaporation can speed up or slow down depending on temperature. When the temperature is cool, the rate of evaporation is slower.

A puddle of water will take longer to evaporate on a cold day than it will on a warm day.

The rate of evaporation is faster when the temperature is higher.

Washing hung on a washing line will dry quicker on a warm day than it would on a cool day because water evaporates from the wet washing at a faster rate when it is warmer.

Working Scientifically

Observe the rate of evaporation at different temperatures by placing open containers with water (all the same size and all with the same volume of water) in locations with different temperatures. Record any changes over a period of a few days and explain what you have found.

Quick Test

1. Name three types of precipitation.
2. What is the process called when water vapour rises from a body of water?
3. What would you notice about a puddle on a cool day and a puddle in the same place on a warm day?
4. How do clouds form?

Key Word

- Precipitation

45

Practice Questions

1 What are the **three** states of matter?

_____ _____ _____

3 marks

2 Match each material below to its state of matter.

| Wood | Orange juice | Oxygen |

| Gas | Liquid | Solid |

3 marks

3 Why does washing on a line dry faster on a warm day than on a cool day?

_____

1 mark

1 Complete the labels on the water cycle diagram below.

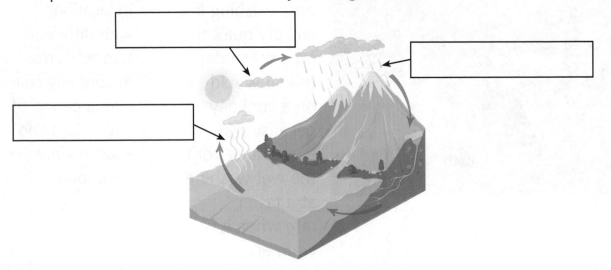

3 marks

1 Explain what happens when water vapour from the ocean cools in the air.

_____

1 mark

2 Explain what happens to a liquid during the process of evaporation.

_____

1 mark

3 What will happen to the volume of a gas if it is released from a small bottle into a large box?

_____

1 mark

Review Questions

1   Why do most animal babies look like their parents?

_____

1 mark

2   True or false? All offspring from the same parents will inherit all of the same characteristics? _____

1 mark

3   What are differences between a group of the same species known as? Circle **one**.

    adaptations   inheritances   variations   evolutions

1 mark

4   Bruce is tall, has blonde hair and enjoys singing and playing football. Which of these characteristics could he have inherited from his parents?

_____

2 marks

5   Why do living things need to adapt to their environments?

_____

1 mark

6   Give **one** example of how a camel is adapted to living in the desert.

_____

1 mark

7   True or false? Humans have never evolved. _____

1 mark

8   Is it possible for different animals to evolve from one ancestor? _____

1 mark

9   What makes animals evolve differently?

_____

_____

2 marks

10 What can scientists look at that show how plants and animals used to look millions of years ago? _____

1 mark

11 Is it possible to tell when a fossil was formed? How?

_____

2 marks

Properties and Uses of Materials

- Compare and group materials on the basis of their properties
- Give reasons for the particular uses of everyday materials

Materials can be grouped according to their properties. This is important because it helps people make decisions about which material is best for a particular job.

Hardness: some materials are hard and some are soft.

- Hard materials are difficult to break, bend or scratch and are used if something needs to be really tough.
- Soft materials are used when flexibility and softness is important.

Solubility: some materials dissolve in water.

- Soluble materials dissolve and are useful for food and medical products.
- Insoluble materials will not dissolve and are needed if products are to be used with water.

Transparency: some materials are see-through.

- Transparent (see-through) materials are needed for a range of purposes.
- When transparency is not needed, opaque materials (which cannot be seen through) are used.

Tip

Remember – many materials have more than one property. This needs to be considered when deciding whether a material is suitable for a purpose.

Working Scientifically

Create an enquiry to work out which materials are best for a certain job, for example, insulating an ice cube to reduce the rate of melting. Consider the equipment you will need and how it will be a fair test.

Conductivity of heat: some materials let heat flow through.

A thermal conductor lets heat travel through it and is used when heat needs transporting to another place. Metals are good conductors of heat. A metal saucepan conducts heat to the food inside it. A metal radiator conducts heat from the hot water inside it to the air on the outside. Heat cannot pass through a thermal insulator, which is used for keeping heat in or out. Wood is not a good conductor of heat, and so a wooden spoon insulates against heat when stirring hot liquids. Many fabrics are good insulators and help prevent heat from our body being lost on a cold day.

Conductors of electricity: some materials let electricty flow through.

- An electricity conductor lets electricty flow through it and is used when electricity needs to be transported from one place to another. Metals, such as copper wires, are excellent conductors of electricity.
- An electricity insulator prevents the flow of electricity and is used to prevent accidental contact with electricty. Plastic coating around wires and cables is a good insulator.

Key Point

Heat always travels from warmer materials to colder materials as it tries to balance each material at the same temperature. Heat from inside a radiator will travel through the metal to the cooler air outside the radiator.

Tip

Water conducts electricity. Never touch electrical items with wet hands.

Quick Test

1. Why is diamond sometimes used for tool blades?
2. Why should you avoid touching electrical items with wet hands?
3. Match each material to a use and explain your choice.

   glass   wood   copper   foam

   car seat   pan handle   greenhouse   electrical wire

Key Words

- Soluble
- Insoluble
- Transparent
- Opaque
- Conductor
- Insulator

Reversible Changes

- Demonstrate that dissolving, mixing and changes of state are reversible
- Know that some materials will dissolve in liquid to form a solution
- Describe how to recover a substance from a solution
- Use knowledge of solids, liquids and gases to decide how mixtures might be separated

When different materials are mixed together they can usually be separated again. Some materials change when they are mixed, but sometimes these changes are reversible. There are four main processes for separating mixtures.

Filtering and Sieving

The process of mixing solids and liquids can be reversed by filtering. When a mixture is poured through a filter, the liquid passes through but the solids do not. This process is usually used for separating solids from water (often with several layers of different filters). Filters (such as filter paper) contain many small holes.

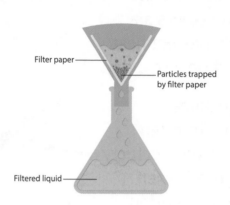

Filter paper

Particles trapped by filter paper

Filtered liquid

Sieving separates larger solids from smaller solids. It is often used to separate objects such as stones from soil, or lumps from flour when baking. The smaller solids pass through the sieve.

Evaporation and Condensation

Some solids dissolve in a liquid to form a solution (e.g. salt water is a salt solution – salt dissolved in water). Sugar dissolves in water too – sweet drinks can contain lots of sugar, but you cannot see it.

Tip

Make sure you choose the right method of separation for the mixture you have: sieving, filtering, evaporation or condensation, or a combination of these.

Key Point

Filters and sieves have different sizes of 'holes'. Very fine holes trap more solids.

Working Scientifically

Investigate the solubility of different materials by placing them in water. Do they dissolve?

issolving is a reversible change. or example, evaporating a salt olution by gently heating it will ave behind the solid (salt) as the ater turns to water vapour.

the water from the solution is lso needed, it must be cooled as evaporates. The condensation an then be collected.

Changes of State are Reversible Changes

ll changes of state can be reversed.

For example, when chocolate gets warm it melts, but it will set hard when it cools again.

The water cycle is a very good example of changes of state being eversible. Water evaporates into water vapour before ondensing back into liquid water.

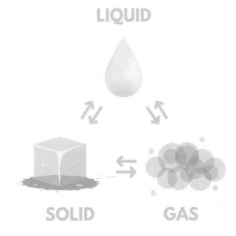

LIQUID

SOLID   GAS

Study

Working Scientifically

Separate a mixture of stones, sand, salt and water. Consider how the materials are mixed. More than one method of separation will be required. Can you explain how and why you are using each method?

Quick Test

1. What process can be used to separate solids from a liquid?
2. How could you separate solids of different sizes mixed together?
3. What is a salt solution?

Key Words

- Dissolve
- Solution

Irreversible Changes

- Explain that some changes result in the formation of new materials and by-products, and that this kind of change is not usually reversible
- Understand that this includes burning and the action of acid on bicarbonate of soda

Some changes are reversible:

- mixing different-sized solids such as stones and sand
- dissolving
- changing states of matter.

But other changes are irreversible. This means that:

- they cannot be undone
- a new material is formed (for example, bread when flour and water are mixed and heated).

Irreversible Changes

Burning fuel	Making bread	Rusting metal

Once burned, the wood has gone forever. It becomes ash.	Once mixed and baked, the ingredients are permanently changed.	Once it has rusted, that part of the metal no longer exists as pure metal.

When some materials are heated, they burn. This causes the material to change. For example, burning wood or charcoal eventually changes it into ash. The ash cannot be changed back into the wood or charcoal. Burning can be very useful though – when a fuel, such as wood, or even oil, is burned, heat and light are given off which can be used for cooking, lighting and providing the energy for transport.

Heating and firing clay, after it has been shaped into cups and plates, is another irreversible change. The heat causes the clay to dry out and harden and, once this has happened, it cannot change back to wet, soft clay again.

Heating food during cooking can also cause irreversible change. The heat provides energy for the change to take place. A boiled egg cannot be changed back into a raw egg.

When some ingredients are mixed together (for example, flour, eggs and milk for pancakes), they cannot be separated. Cooking (providing heat energy) helps this change to become completely irreversible. A pancake would not be very nice if it turned back into flour, raw eggs and milk.

Another way irreversible change happens is when a **reaction** occurs. For example, when iron (a metal) is exposed to oxygen and water for long enough something known as oxidation occurs, which causes rust to form. The rust is a new material and this is an irreversible change – the part of the metal that rusted is gone forever.

Other chemical reactions are useful. Mixing bicarbonate of soda (baking soda) with vinegar or milk causes a reaction – the mixture will bubble as carbon dioxide gas is produced. This change is irreversible – the carbon dioxide cannot be changed back into vinegar and baking soda. This reaction can be used to help baked products rise.

Study

Working Scientifically

Investigate what happens when vinegar and bicarbonate of soda are mixed. Use a bowl and record observations for different amounts of the two materials mixed together. What proportion of vinegar and bicarbonate of soda creates the most fizzing? (You might want to record the length of time the mixture fizzes for.)

Quick Test

1. What happens when iron is exposed to the air and water?
2. Bicarbonate of soda and vinegar _____ when mixed together.
3. Irreversible change means that _____
   _____.

Key Word

- Reaction

Practice Questions

Challenge 1

1   Which material would be most suitable for a scarf? Circle **one**.

    fabric   wood   metal   plastic

    1 mark

2   What process could be used to separate two solids such as stones and soil?

    _____

    1 mark

3   True or false? Melting of chocolate is a reversible change. _____

    1 mark

Challenge 2

1   What happens to iron if it is exposed to oxygen and moisture for too long?

    _____

    1 mark

2   Why is it important that washing powder is soluble?

    _____

    _____

    1 mark

3   Give an example of how burning is a useful irreversible change.

    _____

    1 mark

Challenge 3

WS 1   On a class trip, the children collect some samples of water from a river. They can see that the water is not clean because it has lots of small particles in it. They used the equipment shown below. Explain the method of their enquiry.

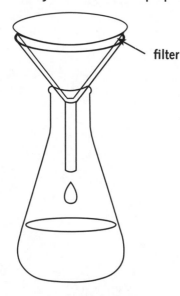

filter

_____

_____

_____

_____

3 mark

Review Questions

1 Which of the following materials are liquid?   sugar   oil   oxygen   water

_____   _____

2 marks

2 In which states of matter do materials change shape depending on their container?

_____   _____

2 marks

3 What happens to a liquid when it is frozen?

_____

1 mark

4 Water vapour cools and turns back into liquid droplets of water. What process is this?

_____

1 mark

5 Name **three** different solids.

_____   _____   _____

3 marks

6 Name **three** different liquids.

_____   _____   _____

3 marks

7 True or false? Precipitation is when water vapour rises from a body of water as it warms.

_____

1 mark

8 True or false? On a warm, dry day a puddle evaporates more quickly than on a wet day.

_____

1 mark

9 What is the process called when a material changes from a solid to a liquid?

_____

1 mark

10 Rain, snow and hail are forms of what?

_____

1 mark

Rocks and Soil

- Compare and group rocks and recognise that soil is made from rocks and organic matter
- Describe how fossils are formed

Rocks

There are three different types of rock, which are all formed in different ways.

Sedimentary rock, e.g. limestone, sandstone, chalk and coal:

- Made from lots of small pieces of materials.
- Formed when plant and animal remains, sand, mud and other small rocks get compressed (squashed together) over time.

Igneous rock, e.g. basalt, granite and pumice:

- Made from melted rocks and minerals.
- Formed when magma cools.

Metamorphic rock, e.g. marble, slate and anthracite:

- Made from igneous or sedimentary rock.
- Formed when rock is heated to high temperatures and compressed under great pressure.

Key Point

There are three main types of rock which have many different varieties. Each variety can look very different and have different properties. The different properties of each rock make them useful for different jobs.

Key Point

Permeable materials allow water to pass through them; impermeable materials do not.

Properties of Rocks

Some rocks, like granite and marble, are tough and strong and are useful for building.

Other rocks, like chalk and sandstone, are softer, and break apart more easily. Chalk can be used as a writing tool because it is so soft.

Some softer rocks, like limestone, are permeable, while other harder ones like slate are impermeable. Impermeable rocks can be used for roofs.

Fossils

Fossils are mostly found in sedimentary rock.

How Fossils are Formed

1. A plant or animal dies.
2. It sinks to the ground and slowly gets covered in mud and sand.
3. Over time, the mud and sand are compressed and a layer of rock is formed.
4. Eventually, a cast (print) of the plant or animal is left in the rock.

Soil

Soil is a mixture of four main things:
1. particles of rock, like sand or clay
2. organic material (decayed plants and animals)
3. water   4. air.

The properties and texture of soil change depending on the amount of sand or clay it contains. Soil is heavier and stickier when it contains more clay and water.

Quick Test

1. What word describes rocks that allow water to pass through them called?

2. What is made when the remains of a plant or animal are imprinted in rock?

3. Complete the sentence: Soil is made of four things: organic material, water, air and _____.

The Solar System

• Describe the shape and movements of the Sun, Moon, Earth and other planets within the solar system

The Solar System

Our solar system has eight **planets**.

The **Sun** is not a planet but a **star** at the centre of the solar system. It gives heat and light to the planets.

All eight planets and the Sun are roughly spherical in shape (like a ball).

The planets always stay in the same order from the Sun: Mercury, Venus, Earth, Mars, Jupiter, Saturn, Uranus and Neptune.

Many other things are moving around in the solar system such as moons, comets, dwarf planets, like Pluto, and asteroids.

Orbiting Planets

The Sun is much bigger than the planets and has a greater **gravitational pull**.

Gravity from the Sun keeps the planets, including the Earth, in **orbit**. This means that they move around the Sun in an elliptical path.

The Earth takes approximately 365 days (one year) to orbit the Sun fully.

All the planets take a different amount of time to orbit the Sun; the further a planet is from the Sun, the longer it will take.

The Moon

Like many other planets, the Earth has a **moon**.

- The Moon orbits the Earth.
- The Moon is a small celestial body (natural body of rock) and not a planet.
- The Earth's gravity keeps the Moon in orbit.
- It takes approximately 28 days for the Moon to orbit the Earth.
- The Moon looks bright but does not produce light; it just **reflects** the light from the Sun.

The Moon, like the Earth and the planets, is spherical, but when it is in different positions around the Earth, it can look different. This happens because, as the Moon orbits the Earth, the Sun's rays illuminate different parts of the Moon and it looks as if the Moon is changing shape.

Working Scientifically

Which planet do you think will orbit the Sun the quickest? Write down your prediction and then use books (a local library will have lots) or the internet to check if you were correct.

Key Point

All the planets orbit the Sun, and the Moon orbits the Earth.

Key Words

- Planets
- Sun
- Star
- Gravitational pull
- Gravity
- Orbit
- Moon
- Reflects

Quick Test

1. How many planets are there in our solar system?
2. What shape are the Sun, Moon and planets?
3. Fill in the gaps in the sentence: The Moon _____ the Earth and the Earth orbits the _____.
4. True or false? The Moon produces light.

Day and Night

• Understand that day and night and the apparent movement of the Sun across the sky are a result of the Earth's rotation

Day and Night

While the Earth is orbiting the Sun, it is also **rotating** around an imaginary line between the North and South Poles called an **axis**. It takes around 24 hours (one day) for the Earth to make a full turn on its axis.

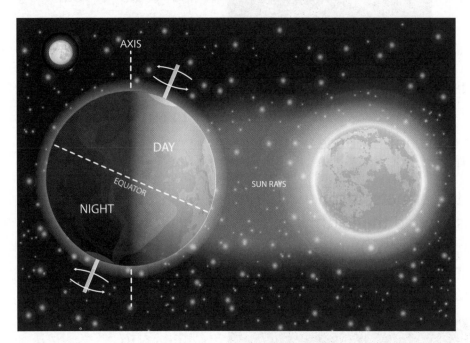

When one side of the Earth is facing the Sun, it receives warmth and light (day time). On the other side of the Earth, it is darker and cooler (night time). The Earth is always rotating, gradually changing which places are experiencing day and night. The amount of time a place spends in the light and dark changes throughout the year. Day times are longer in the summer and shorter in the winter.

The axis of the Earth is slightly tilted (not vertical), which has an impact on the seasons and the amount of daylight.

Key Point

At the **equator**, the Earth rotates at around 1000 miles per hour!

Working Scientifically

See the effect of day and night for yourself. Resources: torch; ball; sticker and a dark room.
1. Put the sticker on the ball.
2. Position the torch to shine the light on the ball.
3. Slowly turn the ball clockwise. What happens to the sticker as you rotate the object? Draw a diagram to show what you found.

Sunrise and Sunset

During the day, the Sun appears to move across the sky, rising in the East and setting in the West. In fact, the Sun is not moving at all. It appears to move because the Earth is continuously rotating.

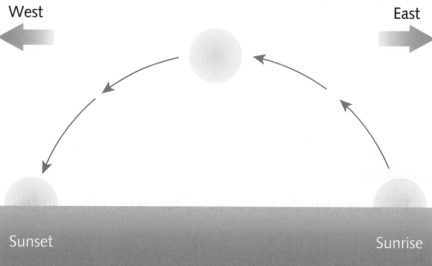

At sunrise, some parts of the Earth are rotating towards the Sun. This makes it look like the Sun is rising into the sky.

Throughout the day, the Earth continues to rotate; at midday, the Sun is at the highest point in the sky.

At sunset, these parts are rotating away from the Sun, and it appears that the Sun is going down.

Before modern watches and clocks were invented, people used to use the position of the Sun in the sky and lengths of shadows to tell what time of day it was.

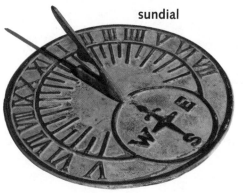

sundial

Instruments called sundials were also made, and people could tell the time by the length and position of the shadows created on these dials.

Key Point

Shadows are longest at sunrise and sunset and shortest at midday.

Key Point

The Sun does not move; the Earth rotates, which changes the position of the Sun in the sky.

Quick Test

1. What imaginary line runs between the North and South Poles?
2. Complete this sentence: Day and night happen because the Earth is _____.
3. True or false? Day time and night time are always 12 hours each.
4. Why does the Sun appear to move across the sky?
5. What is one way that people measured time before clocks were invented?

Key Words

- Rotating
- Axis
- Equator

Practice Questions

Challenge 1

1   Which of the following is a property of some types of rock? Tick **one**.

sedimentary ☐   permeable ☐

igneous ☐   metamorphic ☐

1 mark

2   Are there eight or nine planets in our solar system? _____

1 mark

3   True or false? The Sun orbits the planets in the solar system. _____

1 mark

Challenge 2

1   Order the stages of fossil formation by numbering them 1–4.

A shape or imprint of the plant or animal is formed in the rock.   ☐

A plant or animal dies.   ☐

The layers become compressed and form rock over and around
the plant or animal.   ☐

Over time, the plant or animal gets covered by sand and mud.   ☐

4 marks

2   Name **three** planets from our solar system.

_____   _____   _____

3 marks

3   Describe the way the Moon moves around the Earth.

_____

_____

_____

2 marks

Challenge 3

1   At school, some younger children are talking about how the Sun moves
across the sky. Explain what happens and why it looks like the Sun
is moving.

_____

_____

_____

_____

_____

_____

3 marks

Review Questions

1   Which of the following materials are hard?

foam   diamond   cotton   iron

_____

2 marks

2   Why can it be dangerous to touch an electrical device or switch with wet hands?

_____

1 mark

3   What happens to sugar when it is added to water?

_____

1 mark

4   Complete this sentence:
If a material does not dissolve it is said to be _____.

1 mark

5   What equipment could be used to separate a mix of large and small gravel pieces? _____

1 mark

6   Which of the following are soluble in water?
salt   sand   sugar   steel

_____

2 marks

7   True or false? Wood is a good thermal insulator. _____

1 mark

8   True or false? Dissolving salt in water is an irreversible change. _____

1 mark

9   How is the process of evaporation of water reversed?

_____

1 mark

10 How could salt be separated from a salt solution?

_____

1 mark

Light and Dark

- Recognise that light is needed to be able to see and understand that darkness is the absence of light
- Understand that some light, such as sunlight, can be dangerous to the eye
- Notice that light is reflected from surfaces

Light and Dark

Light is a form of energy. It is needed to be able to see; when it is dark, it is difficult to see. Darkness happens when there is little or no light.

Sources of Light

A light source is something that makes light. Light sources can be either natural or artificial.

Natural:

Sun　　　Lightning　　　Fire

Artificial:

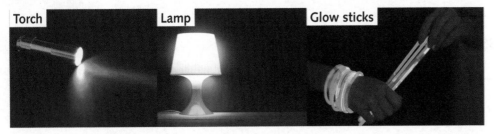
Torch　　　Lamp　　　Glow sticks

Artificial light sources need a supply of energy. This usually comes from batteries or mains electricity (electricity provided through electrical sockets), although some sources, such as glow sticks and fireworks, get their energy from chemical reactions.

Key Point

Some plants and animals can produce light, such as fireflies, jellyfish and some types of mushrooms.

Working Scientifically

Have a look around your home. What light sources can you find? Are there more natural or artificial sources of light?

Key Point

Light comes from lots of different sources and is needed to be able to see.

The Sun

The Sun is the most powerful source of natural light. It is vital to life on Earth.

Light from the Sun is so powerful that it can be dangerous and can damage the eye. It is important to protect the eyes from the Sun and to never look directly at it.

Wearing sunglasses or a sunhat and staying in the shade are simple and effective ways to protect the eyes.

Light Reflects

Light can be reflected off the surfaces of the objects around it.
Light reflected from an object allows us to see.
Light reflects from a surface at the same angle that it hits it.

Smooth, bright, lightly-coloured and shiny materials and objects, like mirrors, reflect almost all the light that falls on to them. Some special fabrics also reflect a lot of light and can be used to make clothing that can be seen more easily in the dark.

Dull, dark and rough materials do not reflect the light as well, and absorb some of the light energy.

Tip

To protect your eyes, follow these three steps:
1. Never look directly at the Sun.
2. Do not shine lights directly into the eye.
3. Wear sunhats and sunglasses in bright sunlight.

Key Point

Light can be reflected and will reflect from the objects it falls on.

Quick Test

1. True or false? Light is necessary to be able to see.
2. Name two natural sources of light.
3. Name two ways that our eyes can be protected from the Sun.
4. Complete the sentence: Light that is not reflected from an object is _____.

Key Words

- Light source
- Artificial

How Light Travels

- Know that light travels in straight lines
- Understand that objects can be seen because they make or reflect light which travels into the eye
- Explain how light travels from a source to help us see things

How Light Travels

Light travels in straight lines. It cannot bend around corners or go around objects by itself.

It also travels extremely quickly; in fact, it is the fastest known thing in the universe.

Unlike sound, light does not need a material to travel through. It can travel in a vacuum. This is important because it means that light from the Sun can travel through space to the Earth.

How Objects are Seen

Sometimes, light produced by a source travels directly to the eye allowing us to see the object. The light made by a fire, for example, travels in straight lines into the eye.

Objects that do not produce light themselves can be seen because they reflect light from another source.

Key Point

Light travels very quickly in straight lines and cannot bend around corners.

Key Point

Objects are seen because they produce or reflect light that travels to the eye.

In the diagram, light travels from the Sun to the ball; it is reflected and then travels into the eye.

Once light enters the eye, a message is sent to the brain, and the brain interprets what it is seeing.

Using Reflection

Light travels in straight lines and cannot bend around corners or change direction by itself. However, it is possible to use reflective objects, like mirrors, to reflect light, changing its direction and making it possible to see things that are normally out of sight.

Reflection is useful in everyday life.

A periscope is a piece of equipment used to see things that are normally out of sight. Periscopes are used in submarines to see what is happening above the water.

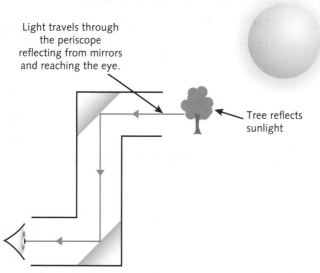

Light travels through the periscope reflecting from mirrors and reaching the eye.

Tree reflects sunlight

Key Point

Mirrors are so smooth and shiny, they reflect all the light that falls on them. This is why objects can be seen reflected in them and why they can be used to see objects which would normally be out of sight.

Working Scientifically

Design and make your own periscope to see around a corner. You will need at least two mirrors and some cardboard tubes.

Quick Test

1. In what sort of pathway does light travel?
2. True or false? We see things because we send out light from our eyes to objects.
3. How do we see the light from a candle?
4. What can be used to help us see things that are out of sight, such as behind us or around a corner?
5. Give an example of how mirrors are used in everyday life.

Key Words

- Eye
- Brain
- Reflection
- Periscope

Shadows

- Recognise that shadows are formed when an opaque object blocks light
- Find patterns in the way shadows change in size

Transparent, Translucent and Opaque

Objects made from different materials allow different amounts of light to pass through them. Objects and materials can be:

Transparent: allowing all or most light to travel through. It is possible to see clearly through transparent materials, e.g. glass, water and air.

Translucent: allowing some light to pass through. It is not possible to see through translucent objects, e.g. tissue paper, frosted glass and many fabrics.

Opaque: blocking all light from passing through. It is not possible to see through opaque objects at all, e.g. wood, stone and metal. Opaque materials create shadows when they block light.

Key Point

Shadows are made when an opaque object blocks light from a source.

Shadows

Shadows are dark shapes which are made when an opaque object blocks light from a source.

A shadow will usually be a similar shape to the object that made it.

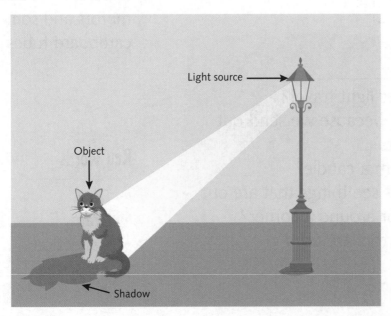

Light source

Object

Shadow

Changing Shadows

While the shape of a shadow will usually be similar to the object that made it, it can be changed and distorted. The size of a shadow can change depending on the distance of the object from the light source or the position of the light source in relation to the object.

Objects which are closer to the light source block more light and make bigger shadows.

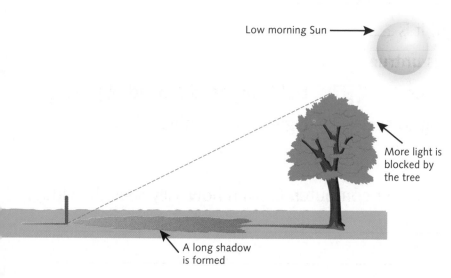

Low morning Sun ⟶

More light is blocked by the tree

A long shadow is formed

Shadows made in the morning and evening are much longer than shadows made at midday. This is because the Sun is lower in the sky in the morning and evening so the person or object will be blocking more light and making a bigger shadow. At midday, the Sun is overhead so less light is being blocked and the shadow is smaller.

Quick Test

1. Which word describes a material or object that allows most or all light to pass through it called?
2. Which word describes objects or materials that create shadows?
3. True or false? A shadow is usually the same shape as the object that made it.
4. Which will make a bigger shadow: an object that is close to the light source or an object that is further away?
5. Shadows can change when the light source is closer or further away. How else can the size of a shadow be changed?

Practice Questions

Challenge 1

1   Use the words provided to complete the sentences.

> light   see   dark

a) To be able to _____ we need _____.

2 marks

b) When there is no light it is _____.

1 mark

2   Tick the statement that is **untrue**.

Light travels in straight lines. ☐   Light can bend around objects. ☐

Without light, it is difficult to see. ☐   Light can be reflected. ☐

1 mark

Challenge 2

1   Tilly is looking at a video on her computer. Explain how Tilly sees the video.

_____

_____

2 marks

2   Name **one** natural and **one** artificial source of light.

_____   _____

2 marks

3   What happens when an opaque object blocks the light from a source?

_____

1 mark

Challenge 3

1   Harry can see a statue from his bedroom window. He notices that he can
only see it during the day and that the shadow it makes changes in size.

a) How is it possible for Harry to see the statue during the day?

_____

_____

3 marks

b) Why can Harry not see the statue at night?

_____

_____

2 marks

c) Why does the statue's shadow change during the day?

_____

_____

2 marks

Review Questions

1   Which type of rock is made when small stones, sand and mud get compressed together?

   _____
   1 mark

2   What word describes a rock that does not allow water to pass through it?

   _____
   1 mark

3   Basalt, granite and pumice are all examples of which type of rock?

   _____
   1 mark

4   Fossils are most likely to be found in which type of rock?

   _____
   1 mark

5   Name **two** things that soil is made from.

   _____   _____
   1 mark

6   Which type of mud is thick, heavy and sticky and can be rolled into a sausage shape?

   _____
   1 mark

7   In our solar system, which is the **third** planet from the Sun?

   _____
   1 mark

8   The Sun, the Earth and the Moon are all the same shape.
   What shape are they?

   _____
   1 mark

9   What force keeps the planets in orbit around the Sun?

   _____
   1 mark

10 True or false? The Moon reflects the light from the Sun. _____
   1 mark

11 What does the Earth do that brings about day and night?

   _____
   1 mark

12 How can the position of the Sun be used to tell what time of day it is?

   _____

   _____

   _____
   2 marks

Contact Forces

- Compare how things move on different surfaces and notice that some forces need contact between objects
- Identify the effects of air resistance, water resistance and friction on moving objects

Forces

There are two types of force: pushes and pulls. Forces act on an object to make it move, accelerate, slow down, stop and change shape. Most forces are applied by contact. The unit used to measure forces is the Newton (N).

Pushes   **Pulls**

A force can make an object move, speed up, slow down or change shape.

A force acting in the opposite direction can prevent or reduce these effects.

Whenever objects are moving, there are forces acting against them, including friction, air resistance, water resistance and gravity.

Friction

Friction is a force that acts when one surface is moving against another. It acts in the opposite direction to slow down and stop moving objects.

Rough surfaces such as carpet, sandpaper and tarmac create a lot of friction and slow objects down quickly. Smooth surfaces such as ice, glass and polished materials do not create much friction and do not slow objects down as quickly.

Key Point

Forces are pushes and pulls acting on an object. They can move, accelerate, slow down, stop and change the shape of objects.

Working Scientifically

Friction also produces heat. Try rubbing your hands together. Can you feel them warming up? The heat is generated by the friction of your hands rubbing together.

riction can be very useful in everyday life. The right ombination of surfaces can provide grip, like tyres on the bad, or allow objects to slide, like skis on a snow slope.

Air and Water Resistance

ir and water resistance are forces that affect moving bjects. They act in the opposite direction to the moving bjects to slow them down.

ir resistance occurs when omething is moving hrough the air. For xample, air resistance acts n a parachute to slow eople and objects down s they fall.

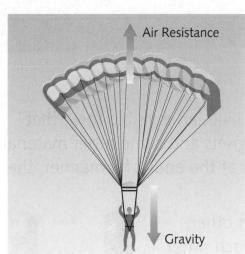

Water resistance occurs hen something is noving through water. For xample, water resistance cts on a boat as it is propelled through the water.

Vide, flat or rough objects travel more slowly through ir and water because they encounter more resistance. treamlined objects are shaped to encounter less resistance nd move more quickly and easily.

   Birds, aeroplanes and race cars are streamlined and can move quickly and easily through the air.
   Sharks, fish and speedboats are streamlined and move quickly and easily through the water.

Vhen an object is in water, another force is also acting on . This is called upthrust, which helps objects to float and an make them appear lighter.

Key Point

Streamlined objects travel more quickly and easily through air and water because there is less resistance. Wide and flat objects have more resistance and move more slowly.

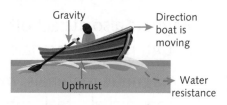

Quick Test

1. What are forces?
2. Which force is usually applied to a shopping trolley?
3. Name a force that can slow an object down.
4. Give an example of an object that is streamlined to lower the air resistance that would slow it down.

Key Words

- Force
- Contact
- Newton
- Friction
- Air resistance
- Water resistance

Magnets and Gravity

- Notice that magnetic forces act from a distance and understand that magnets can attract and repel themselves
- Classify materials that are magnetic and non-magnetic
- Describe magnets as having two poles and predict whether magnets will attract or repel each other
- Explain that unsupported objects fall towards Earth because of gravity

Working Scientifically

If you have a magnet at home, try testing different objects and materials around your house. Which materials are magnetic and which are not? Make a list.

Magnets

Magnets have a magnetic field, an invisible force that attracts or repels other magnets and some other materials. Magnetic force is strongest at the ends of a magnet, the north pole and south pole.

Opposite poles attract each other, and matching poles repel each other.

Magnets also attract other materials, though not all materials:

- magnetic materials: metals such as iron, nickel, steel, cobalt and some minerals like lodestone

- non-magnetic materials: metals such as aluminium and gold as well as most other non-metals such as wood and plastic.

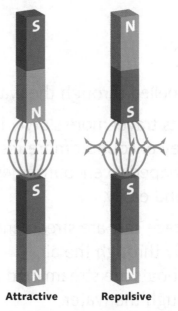

Attractive   **Repulsive**

Key Point

A compass works because the magnetised needle in the compass is attracted to the Earth's magnetic North Pole. The needle acts just like a bar magnet.

Magnetic Force

Unlike most other forces, magnets do not need to touch other materials or magnets to apply a force to them. They have a magnetic field around them which can affect any magnetic material within the field.

The iron filings are moved by the magnetic force from the bar magnet

Gravity

Gravity is the force that pulls objects towards the centre of the Earth. Without it, objects would not fall, they would float.

If an object is not supported by something with an equal or greater force, it will fall because it is being pulled toward the ground by gravity.

Example

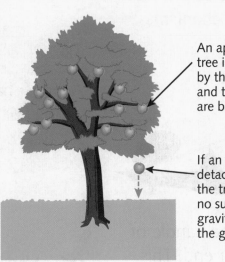

An apple in the tree is supported by the branches and the forces are balanced.

If an apple detaches from the tree, there is no support and gravity pulls it to the ground.

Gravity acts equally all over the Earth and on all objects in its reach, pulling them towards the Earth's centre. This is why people and objects do not fall off the planet.

Study

Key Point

Both magnets and gravity can act from a distance and affect objects without touching them.

Quick Test

1. Name the two ends of a magnet.
2. Circle the correct underlined word/s to complete the sentence: Magnets <u>do/do not</u> need to touch an object to affect it.
3. Where is the strongest point on a magnet?
4. Is gravity a push or a pull force?

Key Words

- Magnets
- Magnetic field
- North pole
- South pole
- Magnetic
- Non-magnetic

Levers, Pulleys and Gears

- Recognise that some mechanisms, including levers, pulleys and gears, allow a smaller force to have a greater effect

Increasing Force

Some jobs, like lifting and moving heavy objects, need a lot of force. To make these jobs easier, it is possible to increase the effect of a smaller force by using simple mechanisms such as levers, pulleys and gears.

Levers

Levers are very simple mechanisms that use a long object like a bar, beam or pole and a pivot.

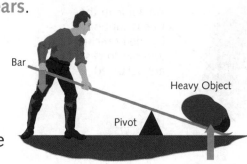

Bar
Heavy Object
Pivot

When a small force, like a push, is applied to the handle of the lever, a larger force is produced at the other end. This means that very heavy objects can be moved and lifted quite easily.

Levers are very useful in daily life; they can look very different, but all work in the same way. Examples of everyday levers include wheelbarrows and seesaws.

Pulleys

A pulley is a rope that runs over a wheel or system of wheels. Pulleys can make jobs easier because they change the direction of the force – it is easier to lift a heavy object by pulling downwards with gravity, than by pulling upwards against gravity.

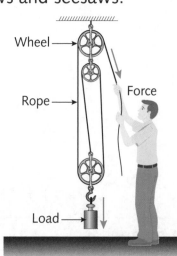

Wheel
Rope
Force
Load

When the rope is pulled down at one end, it lifts the object at the other. With pulleys, it is easier to lift heavy objects, and it is also possible to lift objects higher.

Examples of everyday pulleys include cranes and pulleys on ship sails.

Tip

A longer handle on a lever will make a job easier.

Working Scientifically

Think of a job at home which is hard work, perhaps carrying your toys upstairs. Design a simple mechanism that might help you to make the job easier. Could you use a pulley or a lever?

Gears

Gears are made up of cogs. Cogs are wheels with teeth around the edge. The teeth of one cog fit together with the teeth of other cogs, and when one is turned the others also turn.

Different sized cogs turn at different speeds and need a different amount of force to turn them, for example, a small cog, with fewer teeth, rotates faster and needs less force than a larger cog with more teeth.

Each cog turns in the opposite direction to the cog it is connected to.

Example 1

On a bicycle, gears can be used to change the speed or the force (effort) needed to move the bike.

Example 2

In a clock, different-sized gears are used to turn the hands at different speeds.

Gears are used in lots of different machines.

Gears do not have to be connected to each other directly, they can be connected by a chain (like the gears on a bicycle).

> **Key Point**
>
> Levers, pulleys and gears help to make jobs easier by increasing the effect of a smaller force.

Quick Test

1. Which mechanism uses a pivot?
2. Which mechanisms can be used to lift heavy objects more easily?
3. True or false? A lever with a longer handle will help make lifting easier.
4. Circle the correct underlined word to complete the sentence: Levers, pulleys and gears make jobs easier by increasing/decreasing the effect of a smaller force.

> **Key Words**
>
> * Increase
> * Mechanisms
> * Levers
> * Pulleys
> * Gears
> * Pivot

Practice Questions

Challenge 1

1 Tick the statements about forces which are correct.

They are pushes and pulls. ☐   They all need contact to have an effect. ☐

They are measured in Newtons. ☐   When they are balanced, objects move. ☐

☐
2 marks

2 Use the words from the box to complete the sentences.

> friction   smooth   rough

When two moving objects touch, a force called _____ occurs.

_____ surfaces cause more friction than _____ surfaces.

2 marks

3 True or false? Opposite poles of a magnet will attract each other.

_____

1 mark

Challenge 2

1 Name a force that can act from a distance. _____

1 mark

2 Kinga is watching the snow fall from the sky. Name **two** forces
that are acting on the snow as it falls.

_____   _____

2 marks

WS 3 Charlotte is testing some objects from around the classroom to see if
they are magnetic. Put a tick or cross in the table to show the results you
would expect to see.

Object	Wooden pencil	Steel paperclip	Aluminium can	Plastic straw
Magnetic				

4 marks

Challenge 3

1 Look at the images below. Tick the lever which would make lifting a heavy
object easiest.

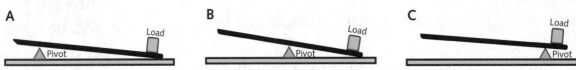

A   B   C

1 mark

2 Mechanisms like levers, pulleys and gears can make difficult jobs easier.
Explain why. _____

1 mark

Review Questions

1 Circle the correct underlined word to complete the sentence.
Light travels in <u>straight</u>/<u>wavy</u> lines.

1 mark

2 What is darkness?

_____

1 mark

3 What is an object that produces light known as?

_____

1 mark

4 Name a natural source of light other than the Sun. _____

1 mark

5 You should never look directly at the Sun. Describe how else you can
keep your eyes safe from bright sunlight.

_____

2 mark

6 What kind of materials reflect light well?

_____

2 mark

7 When light does not pass through an object and is not reflected by it,
what happens to the light?

_____

1 mark

8 What is a material called that allows most or all light to pass through it?
Tick **one**.

transparent ☐   translucent ☐   opaque ☐

1 mark

9 How are shadows formed?

_____

_____

2 mark

10 Complete the sentence: We can see objects that do not produce light
because _____

_____.

2 marks

11 When an opaque object is moved closer to a source of light, what will
happen to its shadow? Circle **one**.

gets smaller   changes shape   gets bigger   no change

1 mark

12 What is the name of the piece of equipment used in submarines to
see above the water? _____

1 mark

Making Sounds

- Identify how sounds are made
- Know that vibrations travel through a medium to the ear
- Understand that sound gets fainter as distance increases

How Sounds Are Made

Sounds are made when an object vibrates. The energy of the vibrations makes a sound wave that travels to the ear. These can be long continuous vibrations like music or short bursts like a knock at the door.

Working Scientifically

Place your fingers gently on the front of your neck and talk, sing or hum. Can you feel the vibrations? Find objects around the home that make a sound. Try and feel for the vibrations.

How Sound Travels

Sound can travel through the air and through lots of different materials (media) including solids (e.g. wood, glass and metal), liquids (e.g. water) and gases (e.g. air) – in fact, it travels faster in solids and liquids. Sound travels in the following way:

- An object vibrates and makes the air or medium around it vibrate.
- The vibrations pass along from one particle to another, through the medium, to the ear.
- The eardrum vibrates, passes a message to the brain, and the sound is heard.

Key Point

Vibrations make sound.

ound cannot travel without a medium (in a **vacuum**). A acuum is a space where there is nothing at all for sound to ravel through, not even air. Sound cannot be heard if there a vacuum between the object vibrating and our ears.

ibrations travel om the clock rough the rrounding air.

The bell jar creates a vacuum so the sound from the clock cannot travel.

ounds and Distance

Vhen a sound is made, the vibrations/sound energy near e object is high, and the sound is louder. As vibrations avel, they lose energy and get smaller, so the sound ecomes fainter (quieter). The further sound travels, the inter it gets.

The music is fainter at the back because the vibrations have travelled and become weaker.

The music is louder at the front because the vibrations are strong.

Quick Test

1. How is sound made?
2. What is the material which sound passes through called?
3. Can sound pass through solids?
4. True or false? Sounds get fainter as distance increases.
5. Finish this statement: Sound cannot travel through a _____.

Key Words

- Vibrations
- Medium
- Vacuum

Pitch and Volume

- Find patterns between the volume of sound and the size of vibrations
- Find patterns between the pitch of a sound and the object producing it

Volume

The **volume** of a sound refers to how loud or quiet it is. Loud noises are made from bigger vibrations with lots of energy, and quiet noises are made from smaller vibrations with less energy.

Banging hard on a drum makes a louder sound because it has more energy and the vibrations are bigger.

Tapping gently on a drum provides less energy, makes smaller vibrations and produces a quieter sound.

High or Low Pitch

The **pitch** of a sound refers to how high or low the sound is. A faster vibration will produce a higher-pitched sound.

- High-pitched sounds include whistling, a small bird chirping and a fire alarm.
- Low-pitched sounds include thunder, a deep voice and a big bass drum.

Changing Pitch

The pitch of a sound depends on the size, length or tension of the object making it. Changes to these things will produce different pitches.

Key Point

More energy ⇨ Bigger vibrations ⇨ Louder sound

Working Scientifically

You can change the volume of your speaking voice – you can shout, talk and whisper. Try and say the same sentence in each different way. Which one needed more effort (energy)? Which was louder?

The mbira [left], is an African musical instrument played by plucking the tines:

- shorter, thinner tines produce high-pitched sounds
- longer, wider tines produce low-pitched sounds.

Study

Another way to change the pitch of something is to adjust the tension (how tight it is).

Guitars are tuned by tightening or loosening the strings. Tighter strings produce a higher-pitched sound.

High-pitched sounds have high-**frequency** sound waves (faster vibrations).

Low-pitched sounds have low-frequency sound waves (slower vibrations).

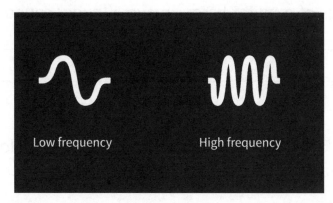

Low frequency   High frequency

Quick Test

1. True or false? Bigger vibrations with more energy make quieter sounds.
2. Will banging harder on a drum change the pitch or the volume?
3. Complete the sentence by circling the correct underlined words: A mouse squeaking is an example of a <u>high-pitched/low-pitched</u> sound.
4. True or false? Changing the length of a guitar string will change the pitch.

Key Words

- Volume
- Pitch
- Frequency

Practice Questions

Challenge 1

1   How are sounds made?

_____

1 mark

2   Circle the correct underlined word to complete the sentence.

Sound cannot travel through a solid/vacuum.

1 mark

3   True or false? Faster vibrations make a lower-pitched sound. _____

1 mark

Challenge 2

1   What part of a guitar makes the sound and how does the sound travel to the ear?

_____

_____

2 marks

2   What does the pitch of a sound depend on?

_____

_____

4 marks

3   Why does plucking the strings of a guitar harder make a louder sound?

_____

_____

2 marks

Challenge 3

1   Oliver loves to watch fireworks but doesn't like the loud bangs. Should he stand nearer to or farther away from the display? Explain your answer.

_____

_____

2 marks

2   Oliver decides that he likes the whistles that the fireworks make more than the bangs. Does he prefer high-pitched or low-pitched sounds? How do you know?

_____

_____

2 marks

Review Questions

1 What unit is force measured in? _____

1 mark

2 Which force is used to move the following objects or do the activities? Write the objects/activities in the correct box. Add one more example to each box.

Shopping trolley   Horse and cart   Riding a bicycle   Putting on socks

Push	Pull

4 marks

3 Mo sets a toy car off from the same ramp without pushing. He rolls it on to three different surfaces: carpet, smooth plastic and rough stone.

a) Why does he use the same ramp and not push the car?

_____

1 mark

b) Which surface do you think the car travelled furthest on? Why?

_____

2 marks

4 Look at the images of the magnets below. Write underneath each pair whether they would **attract** or **repel** each other.

A S N   N S   B N S   S N   C N S   N S

_____   _____   _____

3 marks

5 Some forces need contact with objects to affect them. Name a force other than magnetic that acts on objects without contact.

_____

1 mark

6 Give the name of **three** mechanisms that can increase the effect of a force.

_____   _____   _____

3 marks

7 Which mechanism uses a wheel and a rope?

_____

1 mark

Making Circuits

- Identify common appliances that run on electricity
- Construct a simple series circuit
- Identify whether or not a lamp will light in a series circuit
- Use recognised symbols when representing a simple circuit in a diagram

Types of Electricity

Electricity is needed by many of the appliances and devices we use in everyday life. Some use mains electricity (electricity provided through electrical sockets) and others use batteries (also known as cells).

Mains Electricity, e.g. fridge, TV, light blub

These devices are 'plugged in' (connected) to the mains electricity supply.

Battery Powered, e.g. mobile phone, laptop, electric car

These devices use batteries that are either replaced or recharged by the mains supply; the devices do not need to be 'plugged in' when being used.

Electrical Circuits

Electricity travels (flows) from the power source, through components (e.g. bulbs, buzzers, switches, motors) and back to the power source. It flows in a circuit. The wires and components are all good conductors of electricity.

The electricity can flow when the wires connect the power source to the components and then back from the components to the power source. This is known as a circuit.

Key Point

A circuit must be complete (it must be connected together correctly) for electricity to flow.

The bulb in these circuits will not light because the circuits are not complete (they are not connected correctly).

A wire is not connected to the battery to complete the circuit.

A wire is not connected to the bulb to complete the circuit.

The wires are both connected to the same end of the battery – there is no circuit.

Tip

Remember that every circuit must have a power source, and that there will be a component within the circuit doing a job, for example, a bulb that lights up, a motor that drives something or a buzzer that sounds.

Circuit diagrams

When drawing circuits, circuit diagrams are usually used instead of pictures. This makes it much more simple to show the circuit. Different components have different symbols, and wires are drawn as lines.

Symbols Used in a Circuit Diagram

Battery	—||—	Motor	—(M)—
Bulb	—⊗—	Switch (on position)	—o o—
Buzzer	⊻	Switch (off position)	—o⟋ o—

The circuit diagram below shows the same components as the picture next to it.

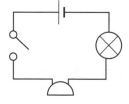

Quick Test

1. What are the two main sources of electricity used in everyday devices and appliances?
2. Complete the sentence: For electricity to flow, a circuit must be _____.
3. Name these components from their symbols:

_____   _____   _____

Breaking Circuits

- Recognise that a switch opens and closes a circuit and associate this with whether or not a lamp lights in a series circuit
- Recognise common conductors and insulators

Switches

A **switch** has the purpose of opening and closing a circuit, sometimes known as making a complete circuit (when the switch is closed) or breaking a circuit (when the switch is open). The switch allows the electricity to flow and can stop that flow.

Key Point

When a switch is closed, it connects two parts of the circuit. The closed switch conducts electricity from one part of the circuit to another.

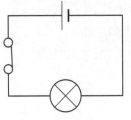

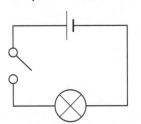

Switch on (closed) – circuit complete – bulb on.

The electricity can flow around the circuit when the switch is pressed (closed). When the switch is open, the circuit is 'broken', the electricity stops flowing and the bulb will not light.

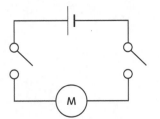

Switch off (open) – circuit broken – bulb off.

The circuit in the diagrams below has two switches. The motor will only work when both switches are on (closed).

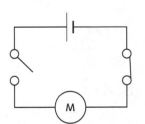

Circuit incomplete – motor not working

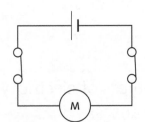

Circuit incomplete – motor not working

Circuit complete – motor working

Conductors and Insulators

All materials are either conductors or insulators.

Conductors allow electricity to pass through them.

Insulators do not allow electricity to pass through them.

The copper wires inside an electrical cable conduct the electricity.

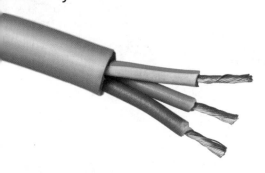

The plastic coatings on each wire and the cable itself are insulators, just as a plastic plug is an insulator, helping make electricity in the home as safe as possible.

Working Scientifically

Investigate different materials to see which are insulators and which are conductors. Create a simple circuit containing a battery and a light bulb. Insert different materials into the circuit to see which conduct electricity (allowing the bulb to light) and which insulate (preventing the bulb from lighting).

Quick Test

1. What does a switch do in a circuit?
2. What is the difference between an insulator and a conductor of electricity?
3. Name a conductor and an insulator of electricity.
4. Why is a plug usually made of plastic or rubber?

Key Words

- Switch
- Conductors
- Insulators

Cells in Circuits

- Associate lamp brightness with the number and voltage of cells
- Compare and give reasons for how components in circuits function

Changing the Performance of Components

All components in a circuit (such as bulbs) rely on electricity. Such components can have their performance changed by allowing more or less electricity to flow to them. As you have seen in the previous pages, using a switch is a simple way to make a component work, or stop it from working, by allowing or preventing movement of electricity around the circuit.

However, there are other ways of changing the performance of components in a circuit.

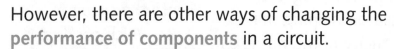

More powerful battery = brighter bulb Using a more powerful battery (a higher voltage battery) in a circuit can make a bulb shine brighter. The circuit diagram simply shows one battery and a bulb. A more powerful battery will also make a buzzer sound louder or a motor run faster.	
More batteries = brighter bulb Adding more batteries into a circuit can also make a bulb shine brighter. Additional batteries (three in total) are shown in the circuit diagram.	
More batteries = louder buzzer Adding more batteries will also make a buzzer sound louder (or a motor run faster).	

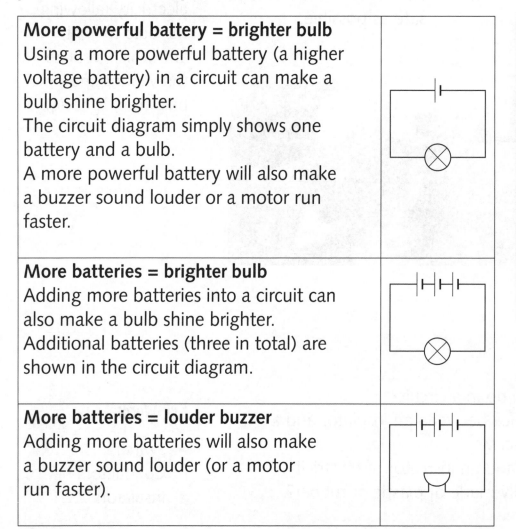

Tip

Always take great care when adding extra batteries or higher powered batteries to circuits. Too much electricity can damage components and stop them working.

More bulbs = dimmer light from each bulb Adding more bulbs into a circuit will make each bulb dimmer as they share the electricity. Three bulbs are shown in the circuit diagram.	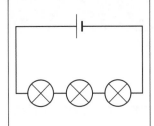
More components = lower performance from each component Just as adding more bulbs into a circuit will make each bulb dimmer, adding further components such as motors or buzzers will reduce their performance as they share the electricity. In the circuit diagram, the bulb, the motor and the buzzer will all have lower performance than they would alone, or than they would if there were just two components in the circuit.	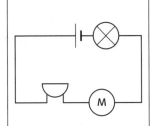

Key Point

Adding more bulbs in a line, one after the other, will make each bulb dimmer as they share the electricity. It is not always necessary to have a motor running at full speed, or a bulb shining at its full brightness and such things are taken into consideration when circuits are designed.

Quick Test

1. What happens to the light from a bulb if a higher-powered battery is used in a circuit?
2. What other change could be made to a circuit to have the same effect on the light?
3. Why should care be taken when using higher powered batteries or extra batteries in a circuit?

Key Words

- Performance of components

Practice Questions

Challenge 1

1 Name **three** appliances or devices that use electricity.

_____   _____   _____

3 marks

2 What component can be used in a circuit to make or break the circuit?

_____

1 mark

3 True or false? Metal is a good conductor of electricity. _____

1 mark

Challenge 2

WS **1** If a simple circuit has one bulb and one battery, what will be the effect of adding an extra bulb?

_____

1 mark

2 Place a tick next to the insulators below. Tick **two**.

wood ☐   metal ☐   plastic ☐   water ☐

2 marks

WS **3** What would happen to the sound from a buzzer if more batteries were added to the circuit?

_____

1 mark

Challenge 3

1 Look at the circuit diagrams below.

Explain which one represents a circuit in which the bulb is lit.

_____

_____

2 marks

Review Questions

1   Finish this sentence. Sounds are made by objects or materials that
    _____.

    1 mark

2   Tick **three** media that sound can travel through.

    air ☐   wood ☐   vacuum ☐   water ☐

    3 marks

3   Which part of the ear detects sound? _____

    1 mark

4   Circle the correct underlined word/s to complete the sentence.

    Smaller vibrations make <u>fainter/lower-pitched</u> sounds.

    1 mark

5   What happens to sound as it travels?

    _____

    1 mark

6   True or false? The word volume describes how high or low the pitch of
    a sound is. _____

    1 mark

7   Smaller, shorter and tighter objects make what kind of sound when
    they vibrate?

    _____

    1 mark

8   True or false? Loosening the skin of a drum will make a
    lower-pitched sound. _____

    1 mark

9   Circle the correct underlined word to complete the sentence.

    An object that is vibrating faster will make a <u>higher/lower</u>-pitched sound
    than one vibrating slowly.

    1 mark

10 True or false? Guitarists change the tension (tightness) of the strings to
    change the volume of their guitar. _____

    1 mark

Review Questions

1   Which of the following materials are conductors of electricity?

    copper   rubber   water   wood

    _____

    2 marks

2   Why are electrical wires surrounded by plastic cable?

    _____

    1 mark

3   Should wires in a circuit usually be connected to the same end of the battery or different ends?

    _____

    1 mark

4   Why should you not push a metal object into an electrical socket or device?

    _____

    1 mark

5   If too much electricity is passed through a component such as a bulb, what will happen?

    _____

    1 mark

6   Adding an extra motor into a circuit already containing a motor will make both motors turn…

    slower ☐   faster ☐

    1 mark

7   True or false? A circuit must be complete for the components in it to work.

    _____

    1 mark

8   Why should you not touch an electrical switch with wet hands?

    _____

    1 mark

9   If a switch in a circuit is open, is the circuit complete? Explain your answer.

    _____

    _____

    2 marks

10 True or false? All electrical circuits must have a source of power.

    _____

    1 mark

1 Indicate whether each member of the food chain below is a producer or consumer.

_____   _____   _____

3 marks

2 A giant panda gets almost all its nutrition from bamboo. Why could this be a problem?

_____

_____

1 mark

3 What is the name of the system that transports oxygen and nutrients around the body? _____

1 mark

4 What is the difference between the way plants and animals find nutrition?

_____

_____

2 marks

5 What is the job of the stomach in the digestive system?

_____

1 mark

6 State **two** jobs of the skeleton. _____

2 marks

7 Which part of the skeleton protects the heart and lungs? _____

1 mark

8 Describe how the muscles in the arm work together to pick up an object.

_____

_____

2 marks

9 Ella is listening to her favourite song on the radio. Explain how she hears the song.

_____

_____

3 marks

10 How do fossils provide evidence to support the theory of evolution?

_____

_____

2 marks

11 Give **two** examples of a camel's adaptations and explain how they help it survive.

_____

_____
2 marks

12 How is metamorphic rock formed?

_____

_____
2 marks

13 True or false? Only animals adapt to their environments. _____
1 mark

WS **14** Stan uses a force meter to test how much force is needed to pull his cart across three different surfaces: carpet, a polished wooden floor and a tarmacked road. He gets three different readings.

Join the readings to the correct surface.

2 Newtons   Carpet

5 Newtons   Tarmac

7 Newtons   Smooth wooden floor
3 marks

15 Karin is watching cars at a race track. He notices that they are a different shape from his Dad's car. Why might this be?

_____

_____
2 marks

16 Name **two** planets that are farther from the Sun than the Earth.

_____   _____
2 marks

17 The planets of our solar system all orbit the Sun. What force keeps the planets in orbit? Give another example of how this force acts.

_____

_____
3 marks

18 One sunny morning, Eva, Jake and Nia are exploring their shadows on the playground. They notice that their shadow stays on one side even when they move or turn around. Explain why their shadows do not change sides when they turn around.

_____

_____
1 mark

19 Why does the Sun appear to move across the sky during the day?

_____

_____

2 marks

20 How does the light from the Sun help us to see?

_____

_____

2 marks

21 Give an example of an artificial source of light. _____

1 mark

22 The Moon is not a source of light. Explain why it is possible to see the Moon at night.

_____

_____

2 marks

23 Circle the mechanism which bicycles use to help make it easier to ride uphill and move faster.

         pulleys   levers   gears

1 mark

24 Look at the picture of the xylophone.

a) Which bar is likely to make the highest-pitched sound? _____

1 mark

b) What effect will tapping the bars harder have on the sound it makes?

_____

1 mark

25 Zac's New Year's resolution is to keep his body healthy. He is already eating a balanced diet. What else can he do to keep his body healthy?

_____

1 mark

26 Write the missing names of the planets in our Solar System.

Mercury _____ _____ Mars   Jupiter _____ Uranus _____

4 marks

WS **27** If an enquiry is trying to find the amount of water to give a plant for the best growth over a two-week period, what variable must be changed?

_____

1 mark

WS **28** An enquiry is trying to find the best material for thermal insulation of a box of ice.

a) Which variables must remain the same?

_____

2 mark

b) Which variable must change?

_____

1 mark

WS **29** Dexter and Uzma repeat a scientific enquiry three times. Why would they do this?

_____

1 mark

30 The pupils observe dandelion seeds being blown by the wind.

a) Why does this happen?

_____

1 mark

b) Name another way in which seeds move away from the plant from which they came.

_____

1 mark

31 What is the difference between the way in which birds are born and the way in which mammals are born?

_____

1 mark

32 What is the main difference between a vertebrate and an invertebrate?

_____

1 mark

33 What happens during the process of pollination?

_____

_____

2 mark

34 Why are leaves and roots so important to plant growth?

_____

_____

2 mark

35 Water turns to water vapour, changing from a liquid to a gas.

What is the name of the process described in the sentence above?

_____

1 mark

36 Match each of the processes below to the correct change of state:

melting   gas to liquid

condensing   liquid to solid

freezing   solid to liquid

2 marks

37 Explain what causes ice to melt.

_____

1 mark

38 Which of the following materials are soluble and which are insoluble?

Add an S or I to the box after each material.

wood ☐   iron ☐   salt ☐   sand ☐   sugar ☐

2 marks

39 Some changes to materials are reversible and some are non-reversible (irreversible).

Say which type of change each change below is.

Cooking an egg is _____.

Melting chocolate is _____.

Dissolving salt is _____.

Rusting of metal is _____.

4 marks

40 Which of the following materials are thermal insulators and which are thermal conductors?

Add a C or an I to the box after each material.

wood ☐   plastic ☐   metal ☐   rubber ☐

3 marks

41 Match each of these methods of separating materials to the mixtures they would be used to separate.

filtering   soil and stones

sieving   sugar dissolved in water

evaporating   sand in water

2 marks

42 Look at the circuit diagram below.

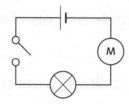

a) What will happen to the bulb when the switch is closed?

_____

1 mark

b) Ali and Jay say the motor will also work when the switch is closed. Are they correct? Explain your answer.

_____

_____

2 marks

43 Explain why the electrical cable below contains copper wires and is surrounded by plastic.

_____

_____

2 marks

44 Bailey is making a model house. The house needs a switch on the outside to turn on two lights in the model.

a) Complete the circuit diagram below so Bailey's circuit works.

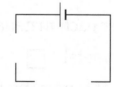

3 marks

b) Bailey decides that the lights need to be brighter. What **two** things could be changed to make this happen?

_____

_____

2 marks

Quick Test Page 5
1 a question
2 the method
3 Fair test means a test in which only the variable being tested is changed, while all other variables remain constant.

Quick Test Page 7
1 the initial amount of snow and the size/shape of the beaker
2 in the airing cupboard
3 to help make sure the data are reliable

Quick Test Page 9
1 it allows patterns or trends in the data to be seen clearly
2 as a line graph
3 The conclusion is a summary of the findings.

Quick Test Page 10
1 to help you reach an accurate conclusion
2 to increase the reliability of data

Practice Questions Page 11
Challenge 1
1 thermometer   1
2 How the enquiry will be done.   1
3 To help keep it tidy and easy to read.   1

Challenge 2
1 different-shaped containers, thermometer (and boiling water), stopwatch/timer, measuring cylinder   1
2 Award one mark for each of the following: Keep the amount of water, the starting temperature of the water and the location the same. Measure the temperature of each at the same time. The only variable that should change is the shape of the container.   3

Challenge 3
1 It can be concluded that the plant on the window sill grew taller (1) because it was in the light (1).   2
2 By repeating the enquiry with more plant samples.   1

Quick Test Page 13
1 a) fish, b) bird, c) amphibian, d) mammal
2 Spiders have eight legs, insects have six; spiders have two body parts, insects have three
3 Vertebrates have a back bone, invertebrates do not

Quick Test Page 15
1 water, light, nutrients, room to grow, air
2 the root and the shoot
3 they produce food for the plant
4 to hold the plant up towards the light, and to transport water to the leaves/food to other parts of the plant

Quick Test Page 17
1 puberty
2 mammals give birth to live offspring which develop outside the body, whereas birds, reptiles and fish lay eggs and the offspring develop in the egg before hatching
3 caterpillar

Quick Test Page 19

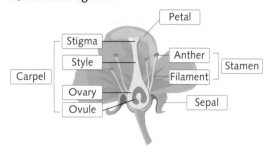

Quick Test Page 21
1 Example answers: pollution, deforestation, habitat destruction, waste, energy generation
2 animals and plants can lose their habitats/habitats are destroyed
3 Habitat creation can help plant and animal life by providing safe places for animals and plants, and by being used to educate people about habitats.

Practice Questions Page 22
Challenge 1
1 An animal with a backbone is called a **vertebrate** and an animal without a backbone is called an **invertebrate**.   2
2 a spider has eight legs and an insect has six legs OR a spider has two body parts and an insect has three   1
3 the root   1

Challenge 2
1 embryo – child – adolescent – adult – old age   1
2 In pollination, pollen from the **anther** sticks to the **stigma**.   2
3 Minerals are important because they help to keep a plant healthy by providing nutrients.   1

Challenge 3
1 Insects, birds, reptiles and amphibians all lay an egg but humans do not.   1
2 The leaves provide the plant with nutrition (food) by using sunlight to change carbon dioxide from the air into food.   1
3 Any two from: by the wind, by animals (sticking to them or by being eaten and then left in excrement), by explosion (seed pods splitting open), carried by water   2

Review Questions Page 23
1 to answer a question, or to prove or disprove an idea (a hypothesis), by testing different things   1
2 the temperature   1
3 Different temperatures need investigating, but all other conditions, e.g. amount of water and type of seed, must remain the same.   1
4 degrees Celsius (°C)   1
5 The given answer must acknowledge that the test is not fair because an additional variable (other than the surface) has been changed (and is not relevant to what is being tested).   1
6 to make sure that the data are reliable   1
7 a) 6 °C   1
   b) The line does not rise as steeply after 12 pm as it did before 12 pm.   1

Answers

Quick Test Page 25
1 producer
2 what something is eaten by
3 An animal that kills and eats another animal is called a **predator**.
4 Animals eat other living things because they cannot make their own food.

Quick Test Page 27
1 digestion
2 small intestine
3 four
4 to cut and slice food
5 around 32

Quick Test Page 29
1 The combination of bones inside a human is called a **skeleton**.
2 to protect the heart and lungs
3 support or movement
4 True
5 When one muscle contracts the other **relaxes**.

Quick Test Page 31
1 to transport oxygen and nutrients around the body and help to get rid of waste
2 The circulatory system is made up of blood, blood vessels and the **heart**.
3 capillaries
4 False
5 in the chest, between the lungs

Quick Test Page 33
1 carbohydrates or energy
2 Eating the right foods, in the right amounts, is known as a **balanced diet**.
3 exercise/stay active, avoid activities or substances which damage the body
4 smoking, drinking alcohol or taking drugs

Practice Questions Page 34
Challenge 1
1 In a food chain, plants are known as **producers** and animals are known as **consumers**. 2
2 the digestive system 1
3 Skeleton = Supports the body and protects organs
Muscles = Work in pairs to help the body move
Heart = Pumps blood around the body 3

Challenge 2
1 Prey – Rabbit   Predator – Fox 2
2 to mix, churn and break down food 1
3 molars and premolars 2

Challenge 3
1 Accept any description that includes: eating a balanced diet and being active, and at least one from avoiding smoking, drinking alcohol and taking drugs. Award 1 mark for each activity. 3

Review Questions Page 35
1 to attract insects 1
2 Water is absorbed from soil by the roots and transported to the leaves by the stem. 1

3 Plants use light to help them make food in their leaves. 1
4 pollen and ovule 2
5 Any two vertebrates, e.g. human and snake, and any two invertebrates, e.g. spider and jellyfish. 4
6 a chrysalis or pupa 1
7 Birds hatch from eggs laid by the female bird. Humans grow inside the body of their mother and are born live. 1
8 In sexual reproduction, an **egg** from the woman is fertilised by a **sperm** from the man. 2
9 Any two forms of pollution, e.g., plastic pollution/plastic waste, air pollution from smoke. 2
10 by providing plants and animals with a safe place and by helping educate people about plants, animals and habitats 2

Quick Test Page 37
1 True
2 hair/eye colour, height, any other physical characteristics
3 variation
4 adaptation

Quick Test Page 39
1 evolution
2 When a living thing has changed over time, we say it has **evolved**.
3 fossils

Practice Questions Page 40
Challenge 1
1 Most **offspring** look like their parents because they **inherit** some of their physical characteristics. 2
2 Cactus = Needle-like leaves to prevent water loss
Duck = Webbed feet for swimming
Bat = Large ears to help navigate in the dark 3
3 True 1

Challenge 2
1 Any two physical characteristics such as hair colour, eye colour, height. 2
2 a) it would find it difficult to survive 1
b) Any two from: transparent fur, webbed feet, a thick layer of fat, black skin 2
3 It is possible to tell the age of a fossil from the rocks they are found in (1). The fossils can then be compared to show how plants and animals have changed over millions of years (1). 2

Challenge 3
1 Accept answers which suggest that giraffes might have developed such long necks to reach the highest branches on the trees. Giraffes with longer necks could reach more leaves and have more food. The giraffes with longer necks survived and passed on this characteristic to their offspring. Over time their necks got longer and longer. Award 2 marks for mention of giraffes with longer necks can reach more food. Award 3 marks for also mentioning survival and passing on characteristics. Award 4 marks for also mentioning long periods of time or many generations. 4

Review Questions page 41
1 consumer 1
2 True 1

3 Tongue and teeth, Oesophagus, Small intestine   3
4 The <u>canine</u> teeth are responsible for tearing and ripping food.   1
5 two   1
6 heart, blood and blood vessels   3
7 Capillaries = Allow oxygen and nutrients to pass from the blood to the body.
   Arteries = Transport blood containing oxygen from the heart to the body.
   Veins = Transport blood containing carbon dioxide to the heart.   3
8 a) fats   1
   b) energy   1
9 Any two from: uses energy from food and reduces fat storage, keeps heart and lungs strong and healthy, improves coordination, improves muscle strength   2
10 Any two from: smoking cigarettes, drinking alcohol, taking drugs   2

Quick Test Page 43
1 0°C
2 evaporation
3 Examples: solid – metal, ice; liquid – water, juice; gas – oxygen, carbon dioxide

Quick Test Page 45
1 e.g. rain, snow and hail
2 evaporation
3 on a warm day it will evaporate more quickly
4 water vapour condenses as it cools in the sky, turning back to droplets of liquid water

Practice Questions Page 46
Challenge 1
1 solid, liquid and gas   3
2 Wood – solid, Orange juice – liquid, Oxygen – gas   3
3 Evaporation is faster when the temperature is higher.   1

Challenge 2
1
Condensation   Precipitation
Evaporation
   3

Challenge 3
1 The water vapour condenses and turns back into liquid water, forming clouds.   1
2 The liquid at the surface is heated by the air and turns into water vapour so the volume of water decreases.   1
3 The volume of the gas will increase to fill the whole box.   1

Review Questions Page 47
1 because they inherit physical characteristics   1
2 False   1
3 variations   1
4 tall, blonde hair   2

5 to survive or make survival easier   1
6 Any one from: fatty hump to store food and water; long eyelashes to protect eyes from sun and sand; soft and wide feet for walking on hot sand; thick fur to protect them from the sun; sandy coloured fur for camouflage   1
7 False   1
8 Yes   1
9 different habitats and mutations   2
10 fossils   1
11 Yes, by dating the layer of rock it was found in.   2

Quick Test Page 49
1 because diamond is very hard and will not wear out quickly
2 You will get an electric shock because water conducts electricity.
3 glass – greenhouse (allows sunlight and heat through); wood – pan handle (thermal insulator so allows a hot pan to be picked up); copper – electrical wire (conducts electricity in a circuit); foam – car seat (soft so comfortable to sit on)

Quick Test Page 51
1 filtering
2 sieving
3 water with salt dissolved in it

Quick Test Page 53
1 it rusts
2 Bicarbonate of soda and vinegar <u>react</u> when mixed together.
3 Irreversible change means that <u>the change is permanent/the change cannot be undone/it cannot be changed back</u>.

Practice Questions Page 54
Challenge 1
1 fabric   1
2 sieving   1
3 True   1

Challenge 2
1 it will rust   1
2 Washing powder needs to be soluble so that it can dissolve in the water and then get to all parts of the washing to clean it.   1
3 When a material is burning, it gives off heat (and light). 1

Challenge 3
1 Award 1 mark for each point: pouring water into the filter paper, water passing through the filter paper into the flask, solid particles being left on the filter paper (being filtered).   3

Review Questions Page 55
1 oil and water   2
2 liquid and gas   2
3 it becomes a solid   1
4 condensation   1
5 Any three solids, e.g. ice, rock, brick, wood, iron, concrete   3
6 Any three liquids, e.g. water, oil, fruit juice, milk, mercury   3
7 False   1

Answers

8	True	1
9	melting	1
10	precipitation	1

Quick Test Page 57
1. permeable
2. a fossil
3. Soil is made of four things: organic material, water, air and **particles of rock**.

Quick Test Page 59
1. eight
2. sphere or spherical
3. The Moon **orbits** the Earth and the Earth orbits the **Sun**.
4. False

Quick Test Page 61
1. axis
2. Day and night happen because the Earth is **rotating**.
3. False
4. because the Earth is rotating
5. by using the position of the Sun in the sky or sundials

Practice Questions Page 62
Challenge 1
1	permeable	1
2	eight	1
3	False	1

Challenge 2
1. 1 A plant or animal dies.
   2 Over time, the plant or animal gets covered by sand and mud.
   3 The layers become compressed and form rock over and around the plant or animal.
   4 A shape or imprint of the plant or animal is formed in the rock. 4
2. Any three from: Mercury, Venus, Earth, Mars, Jupiter, Saturn, Uranus, Neptune 3
3. The gravitational force keeps the Moon in orbit (1). It takes the Moon around 28 days to orbit the Earth (1). 2

Challenge 3
1. The Sun appears to move across the sky because the Earth is rotating (1). The Sun appears to rise in the morning in the East because the Earth turns towards the Sun (1). During the day, the Earth continues to rotate and, by sunset, the same point on Earth is rotating away from the Sun, in the West (1). 3

Review Questions Page 63
1	diamond and iron	2
2	Water conducts electricity so it could result in an electric shock.	1
3	The sugar **dissolves**.	1
4	If a material does not dissolve it is said to be **insoluble**.	1
5	a sieve	1
6	salt and sugar	2
7	True	1
8	False	1
9	by condensation/by condensing the water vapour	1
10	by evaporating the water	1

Quick Test Page 65
1. True
2. Accept any two, e.g. Sun, firefly, lightning, fire
3. Accept two from: don't look directly at it, wear sunglasses and a sunhat, stay in the shade
4. Light that is not reflected from an object is **absorbed**.

Quick Test Page 67
1. in straight lines
2. False
3. The light from the candle travels in a straight line from the candle into the eye. The eye sends a signal to the brain, and the candle is seen.
4. mirror
5. Example answers: mirrors in a car, checking your reflection, dentist mirror, road bend mirror, periscope

Quick Test Page 69
1. transparent
2. opaque
3. True
4. an object that is closer to the light source
5. Shadow sizes can be changed by changing the position of the light in relation to the object. If the light is directly above the object, the shadow will be much smaller. For example, as the position of the Sun changes, the length of a shadow changes.

Practice Questions Page 70
Challenge 1
1	a) To be able to **see** we need **light**.	2
	b) When there is no light it is **dark**.	1
2	Light can bend around objects.	1

Challenge 2
1. The computer produces light which travels to her eye (1). Her eye sends a signal to the brain, and the brain interprets what it is seeing (1). 2
2. Any one natural source, e.g. Sun, lightning, fire, firefly, and any one artificial source, e.g. torch, lightbulb, television, computer 2
3. a shadow is formed 1

Challenge 3
1. a) The light from the Sun reflects off the statue (1) into Harry's eyes (1). The eyes send a signal to the brain, and the brain interprets what it is seeing (1). 3
   b) There is little or no light to be reflected off the statue (1), and the statue does not produce light (1). 2
   c) The shadow will change in size as the Earth rotates and the position of the Sun changes during the day (1). In the morning, the Sun will shine on the side of the statue and the shadow will be longer, at midday the Sun will be directly above the statue and the shadow will be shorter (1). 2

Review Questions page 71
1	sedimentary	1
2	impermeable	1
3	igneous	1
4	sedimentary	1
5	Any two from: water, air, organic material and rock particles	2

6 clay 1
7 Earth 1
8 sphere/spherical 1
9 gravity 1
10 True 1
11 rotates 1
12 At different times of the day, the Sun is in different positions in the sky (1). In the morning, the Sun is low in the sky to the East, at midday the Sun is at its highest point in the sky and in the afternoon, the Sun gets lower in the sky to the west (1). 2

Quick Test Page 73
1 pushes and pulls
2 push
3 friction, air resistance, gravity or water resistance
4 bird, aeroplane, race car, etc.

Quick Test Page 75
1 north and south poles
2 Magnets **do not** need to touch an object to affect it.
3 at the poles
4 pull

Quick Test Page 77
1 lever
2 pulley or lever
3 True
4 Levers, pulleys and gears make jobs easier by **increasing** the effect of a smaller force.

Practice Questions Page 78
Challenge 1
1 They are pushes and pulls and They are measured in Newtons 2
2 When two moving objects touch, a force called **friction** occurs (1). **Rough** surfaces cause more friction than **smooth** surfaces (1). 2
3 True 1

Challenge 2
1 magnetism or gravity 1
2 gravity and air resistance 2
3

Object	Wooden pencil	Steel paperclip	Aluminium can	Plastic straw
Magnetic	✗	✓	✗	✗

4

Challenge 3
1 C 1
2 they increase the effect of a smaller force 1

Review Questions Page 79
1 Light travels in **straight lines**. 1
2 the absence of light 1
3 a light source 1
4 Example answers: fire, fireflies, lightning 1
5 wearing sunglasses and sunhats; staying in the shade 2
6 smooth (1), bright, lightly-coloured and shiny (1) materials 2
7 it is absorbed 1

8 transparent 1
9 Shadows are formed when an opaque object blocks the light from a source. 1 mark for 'blocked light' and 1 mark for the correct use of 'opaque'. 2
10 We can see objects that do not produce light because **light is reflected off the objects and into our eyes (1), the eyes send a signal to the brain, and the brain sees the object (1)**. 2
11 gets bigger 1
12 periscope 1

Quick Test Page 81
1 by a material or object vibrating
2 a medium
3 Yes
4 True
5 Sound cannot travel through a **vacuum**.

Quick Test Page 83
1 False
2 volume
3 A mouse squeaking is an example of a **high-pitched** sound.
4 True

Practice Questions Page 84
Challenge 1
1 by objects vibrating 1
2 Sound cannot travel through a **vacuum**. 1
3 False 1

Challenge 2
1 The strings of the guitar vibrate when they are plucked (1). The vibrations travel through the air to the ear (1). 2
2 Pitch depends on how fast an object vibrates (1) and the length (1), thickness (1) and tightness (1) of the object. 4
3 Plucking harder provides more energy (1), which makes bigger vibrations (1) which make a louder sound. 2

Challenge 3
1 He should stand farther away because the sound gets fainter further from the source. 2
2 High-pitched sounds. The whistles are a higher-pitched sound than the bangs. 2

Review Questions Page 85
1 Newtons 1
2 Push – Shopping trolley and riding a bicycle. Pull – Putting on socks and horse and cart. 4
3 a) to make sure it is a fair test/to control these variables 1

   b) The smooth plastic surface because it will produce less friction. 2
4 A – Repel, B – Repel, C – Attract 3
5 gravity 1
6 levers, pulleys and gears 3
7 pulley 1

Quick Test Page 87
1 mains electricity and battery power
2 For electricity to flow, a circuit must be **complete**.
3 buzzer, motor, bulb

Answers

Quick Test Page 89
1. controls the flow of electricity/makes or breaks the circuit/allows electricity to flow and be stopped
2. An insulator prevents electricity passing through, while a conductor allows electricity to pass through.
3. e.g. conductor – metal; insulator – rubber/plastic
4. to prevent electric shocks as these materials are insulators

Quick Test Page 91
1. the bulb gives a brighter light
2. adding extra batteries/cells
3. too much power could damage/break the components in the circuit

Practice Questions Page 92
Challenge 1
1. Any three battery or mains operated electrical appliances or devices. 3
2. a switch 1
3. True 1

Challenge 2
1. Each bulb will be less bright than the single bulb alone. 1
2. wood, plastic 2
3. It will get louder. (But if too many batteries are added, it could break the buzzer.) 1

Challenge 3
1. The diagram with the switch closed because this completes the circuit and allows electricity to flow. 2

Review Questions Page 93
1. Sounds are made by objects or materials that **vibrate**. 1
2. air, wood, water 3
3. eardrum 1
4. Smaller vibrations make **fainter** sounds. 1
5. it gets quieter/fainter 1
6. False 1
7. high-pitched 1
8. True 1
9. An object that is vibrating faster will make a **higher**-pitched sound than one vibrating slowly. 1
10. False 1

Review Questions Page 94
1. copper and water 2
2. to insulate them, preventing the electricity escaping and giving an electric shock 1
3. different ends 1
4. because it could conduct electricity and cause an electric shock 1
5. it will damage/break the component 1
6. slower 1
7. True 1
8. because water conducts electricity and it could result in an electric shock 1
9. No (1). Because electricity cannot pass through the switch (1). 2
10. True 1

Mixed Questions
1. Grass – Producer: Grasshopper – Consumer: Frog – Consumer 3

2. If there was little or no bamboo, the panda would have no food and would struggle to survive. 1
3. circulatory system 1
4. Plants can make their own food through photosynthesis, they are producers (1). Animals cannot make their own food. They eat other living things, they are consumers (1). 2
5. to mix, churn and break down food 1
6. Any two from: to protect the organs, support the body and help with movement 2
7. ribs/ribcage 1
8. The muscles of the arm work in pairs (1). When one muscle relaxes the other muscle contracts to lift the object (1). 2
9. The radio plays the song and makes a vibration or sound wave (1). The vibrations/sound waves travel through the air to the ear (1). The eardrum receives the sound and sends a signal to the brain and sound is heard (1). 3
10. Fossils show how plants and animals have changed over millions of years. The fossils can be dated (1) and so it is possible to look at plants and animals from millions of years ago and compare them to other fossils and modern living things (1). 2
11. Any two from: long eyelashes to protect from the Sun and sand; sandy coloured fur for camouflage; fatty hump to store food and water; wide soft feet for walking long distances on hot sand; thick fur to protect them from the Sun 2
12. When rock is heated to very high temperatures (1) and put under very high pressure (1). 2
13. False 1
14. 2 Newtons = Polished wooden floor; 5 Newtons = Tarmac; 7 Newtons = Carpet 3
15. To make them more streamlined (1) and to reduce air resistance (1) to help them travel through the air faster. 2
16. Any two from: Mars, Jupiter, Saturn, Uranus and Neptune 2
17. Gravity keeps the planets in orbit (1). Gravity also keeps the Moon orbiting the Earth (1) and pulls objects towards the Earth's centre (1). 3
18. The position of their shadows does not change because the Sun is shining from one side. 1
19. The Sun appears to move across the sky because the Earth is rotating. As the Earth rotates, the Sun appears to move slowly across the sky, rising in the East and setting in the West. 2
20. The light from the Sun reflects off objects in its path into our eyes (1). The eyes send a signal to the brain and the object is seen (1). 2
21. Any artificial light source, e.g. a torch, television, mobile phone, light bulb. 1
22. The Moon reflects the light from the Sun into our eyes. This happens during the day and at night, but it is easier to see at night. 2
23. gears 1
24. a) 1 1
    b) it will make the sound louder 1
25. either stay active/exercise or avoid damage by not smoking, drinking alcohol or taking drugs 1
26. Missing planets in order left to right: Venus, Earth, Saturn and Neptune 4
27. amount of water 1

28 **a)** Award 1 mark for 2 correct answers and 2 marks for 3 correct answers: amount of ice, the box, the temperature   2

   b) the material   1

29 to make their data more reliable   1

30 **a)** to disperse the seeds so they have room to germinate and grow   1

   b) Either carried by animals/stick to animals/eaten by animals, explosion or carried by water   1

31 birds hatch from eggs; mammals are born live   1

32 a vertebrate has a backbone; an invertebrate does not   1

33 1 mark for an acknowledgement that pollen is blown or carried/moves from one plant to another. 2 marks for the additional information that pollen moves from the male part/anther to a female part/stigma.   2

34 1 mark for each:
- roots absorb water [and nutrients] (Also accept that they anchor the plant in the soil.)
- leaves produce food for the plant   2

35 evaporation   1

36 Award 1 mark for one correct answer, 2 marks for all three correct:
melting – solid to liquid; condensing – gas to liquid; freezing – liquid to solid   2

37 Heat warms the ice, turning it to liquid.   1

38 1 mark for two correct answers, 2 marks for all five correct:
Soluble – salt, sugar
Insoluble – wood, iron, sand   2

39 1 mark for each correct answer:
Cooking an egg is irreversible.
Melting chocolate is reversible.
Dissolving salt is reversible.
Rusting of metal is irreversible.   4

40 1 mark for one, 2 marks for two and 3 marks for all four correct:
Conductor – metal; Insulators – wood, plastic, rubber   3

41 1 mark for one, 2 marks for all three correct:
Filtering – sand in water; Sieving – soil and stones; Evaporating – sugar dissolved in water   2

42 **a)** the bulb will light   1

   b) Yes, they are correct (1). The motor is part of the circuit and so electricity will flow through it when the switch is closed (or 'on') (1).   2

43 The copper wires conduct electricity (1). The plastic is an insulator (1) [preventing electricity from getting out].   2

44 **a)** 1 mark for each of a switch and two bulbs correctly drawn and connected.   3

   b) Bailey could add extra batteries (1) or use a more powerful battery (1).   2

Glossary

A

Absorbed — When energy or liquid is taken into another material.

Adaptation — Specific changes to a characteristic of a living thing which help it to survive.

Air resistance — A force, which acts against objects moving through the air and slows them down.

Ancestor — A person, animal or plant that has descendants.

Arteries — Thick, strong blood vessels that carry oxygenated blood around the body.

Artificial — Describes objects made by humans which do not occur naturally.

Asexual reproduction — Reproduction when part of a plant grows into a new plant. (Can also occur in some animals.)

Atrium — Upper chamber or cavity in the heart.

Axis — An imaginary line that runs through the Earth, between the magnetic North and South Poles.

B

Blood — A red liquid which transports water, oxygen, carbon dioxide and nutrients around the body. It is circulated by the heart and blood vessels.

Blood vessels — Small tubes connected to the heart that carry blood around the body.

Brain — A vital organ which allows animals to think and function; protected by the skull.

C

Canines — Sharp, pointed teeth, which can rip and tear tough foods like meat.

Capillaries — Tiny blood vessels that allow nutrients and gases to pass into and out of the blood.

Carbohydrates — Nutrients which provide energy for the body.

Carbon dioxide — A gas produced as a waste product, which is eliminated from the body through the lungs. Carbon dioxide is also present in the air around us and is used by plants to make their food.

Carpel — The female part of a flower

Characteristics — Features or qualities that belong to something, e.g. eye colour, petal colour.

Circuit diagram — A drawing that uses symbols to show how components are connected in an electrical circuit.

Circulatory system — The bodily system consisting of the heart, blood vessels and blood, which delivers oxygen and nutrients to the body and helps eliminate waste such as carbon dioxide.

Classification — Sorting plants and animals into groups based on their features.

Component — Part of an electrical circuit with a specific job, such as a buzzer, bulb or motor.

Conclusion — A summary of the findings of a scientific enquiry.

Condensation — The resulting liquid when a gas is cooled and turns into a liquid.

Conductor — A material which allows heat (thermal conductor) or electricity (electrical conductor) to pass through it.

Consumers — Living things which need to eat other living things to survive. All animals are consumers.

Contact — When any two or more surfaces/objects are touching.

D

Deoxygenated — Containing no oxygen.

Digestive system — Breaks down food into smaller substances the body can use.

Dissolve — A solid dissolves in a liquid when it completely breaks down with no solid particles remaining. This forms a solution, e.g. salt dissolves in water forming a salt solution.

Drugs — Substances which have an effect on the body, e.g. nicotine, alcohol, medicines.

E

Egg — The female reproductive cell in an animal or plant.

Equator — An imaginary line which runs around the middle of the Earth and separates the northern and southern hemispheres.

Evaporation — The process by which a liquid turns into a gas as it is heated.

Evidence — The data or observations from a scientific enquiry.

Evolution — The theory of how living things have changed and adapted over millions of years or many generations.

Eye — The organ which receives light and sends a signal to the brain allowing animals to see.

F

Fair test — A scientific enquiry in which only the variable being investigated changes.

Fats — Nutrients found in foods, such as butter, oils and avocado, which provide the body with energy.

Fertilisation	The process of a sperm (male reproductive cell in animals) or pollen (male reproductive cell in plants) joining with an egg (female reproductive cell).
Fibre	A nutrient found in foods, such as whole grains, nuts and seeds, which keeps the digestive system healthy and moving. Fibre isn't digested easily; it bulks out the waste helping it to move more easily through the intestines.
Food chain	A diagram showing which living things are consumed by others and in which order.
Food web	A group of at least two food chains which are linked by some of the same living things.
Force	A push or pull which can make an object move, accelerate, slow down, stop or change shape.
Fossil	The remains of a plant or animal, which lived millions of years ago, cast into rock.
Freezing	Liquid freezes when it cools to the temperature of its freezing point and becomes a solid.
Frequency	When talking about sound, frequency relates to the speed of a vibration which changes the pitch of a sound. High-frequency produces high-pitched sounds and low-frequency produces low-pitched sounds.
Friction	A force which occurs when one surface is moving against or over another. It always acts against the moving object.

G

Gas	A state of matter which spreads to fill a space.
Gear	A mechanism made from a wheel with teeth around the edge which can lock into other similar mechanisms. Used in bicycles, watches, cars and many other types of machinery.
Generation	People who were born and lived at the same time. Parents are part of one generation and their offspring are part of the next.
Germination	The process of a seedling starting to grow, pushing out a root and shoot.
Gravity	A force which pulls objects towards the centre of a larger object. It keeps the planets orbiting the Sun, the Moon orbiting the Earth and pulls objects towards the Earth's centre.

H

Habitat	The place in which a plant or animal lives.
Heart	A muscular organ which is part of the circulatory system and pumps blood through the blood vessels and around the body.

I

Igneous	A type of rock which is formed when melted rock and minerals (magma) cool and solidify.
Impermeable	A material which does not allow water to pass through it.
Incisors	Sharp, flat teeth at the front of the mouth which cut and slice food.
Increase	To make something bigger.
Inherit	When talking about biology or science, inherit means to get a certain characteristic or set of characteristics from parents.
Insoluble	A material that will not dissolve.
Insulator	A material which will not allow heat (thermal insulator) or electricity (electrical insulator) to pass through it.
Intestines	The organ in the digestive system that breaks down and absorbs nutrients and water. Can be split into the large and small intestines.

K

Kneecap	A small bone at the knee joint which protects the joint and supports movement.

L

Lever	A mechanism consisting of a beam and a pivot which increases the effect of a smaller force and can make lifting or moving heavy objects easier.
Life cycle	The stages of development and decline that a plant or animal goes through during its life, from fertilisation to death.
Ligaments	Short bands which attach the bones of the skeleton at the joints.
Light source	An object which produces light.
Liquid	A state of matter which can be poured and takes the shape of the container it is in.
Lungs	Organs located in the chest which enable animals to breathe.

Glossary

M

Magnet An object which produces a magnetic field and can attract or repel other magnets or magnetic materials.

Magnetic A material or object which is attracted to a magnet.

Magnetic field The area around a magnet in which the magnetic force can act.

Mechanism A simple machine, or part of a machine, which performs an action.

Medium A substance for energy to travel through, e.g. air, water, metal, wood.

Melting The process by which a solid is heated to its freezing point and becomes a liquid.

Metamorphic A type of rock formed when other rocks are heated (not melted) and compressed.

Method How a scientific enquiry is carried out.

Minerals Natural, non-living substances and materials, e.g. metals, diamonds and gems and salts.

Molars Large, wide and flat teeth at the back of the mouth, which crush and grind food.

Moon A moon is a body of natural material like rock which orbits a planet. The Moon refers only to the moon which orbits planet Earth.

Muscles Bands of strong tissue which can contract and relax to move the body.

Mutation A random change to the DNA of a plant or animal.

N

Natural selection When a living thing survives and reproduces because of a specific adaptation, while those without the adaptation do not survive.

Newton (N) The unit in which force is measured.

Non-magnetic An object or material which is unaffected by a magnet.

North/south poles The ends of a magnet where the magnetic force is strongest. It can also refer to the top and bottom of the Earth's axis, which also have a magnetic field.

Nutrients Substances which can be used by a living thing to live, grow and repair, e.g. protein, fats, carbohydrates.

O

Oesophagus A tube in the body which transports food and water from the mouth to the stomach.

Offspring An animal's babies and children.

Omnivore An animal which eats both plants and other animals.

Opaque A material which light cannot pass through.

Orbit To continuously move around in a circular path.

Organic matter/material Material made by the remains of plants or animals.

Ovary Where eggs are made in an animal or plant.

Oxygen A gas in the air which humans and animals need in order to survive.

Oxygenated Something which contains oxygen.

P

Particles Tiny bits of matter, which everything is made from.

Pelvis The large strong bone in the skeleton, which supports the upper body and protects the pelvic organs.

Performance of components The way in which the amount of electricity flowing through a component affects its brightness, volume, speed or other factor.

Periscope An instrument that uses mirrors to reflect light and allow someone to see something which is normally out of sight. Frequently used in submarines to see above the water.

Permeable An object or material which allows water to pass through it.

Pitch How high or low a sound is.

Pivot The part of a lever mechanism which allows the beam or pole to turn or balance.

Planets A large natural object which orbits a star. The planets in our solar system are Mercury, Venus, Earth, Mars, Jupiter, Saturn, Uranus and Neptune.

Pollination The process of pollen getting from an anther (male part) to the stigma (female part) in a flowering plant.

Precipitation Rain, snow or hail falling from the sky.

Predator An animal that hunts, kills and eats other animals.

Premolars Large flat teeth, in front of the molars, which crush and grind food. They develop with the adult teeth.

Prey An animal that is hunted, killed and eaten by another animal.

Producer A green plant that can make its own food.

Protein A nutrient found in food, such as meat and fish, which helps the body to grow and repair.

Puberty	The stage of body changes and development during adolescence (approximately 10–18 years of age in humans).
Pulley	A mechanism consisting of a rope running over a wheel or system of wheels.
Pulse	A wave of pressure, in an artery, which results from the heart beating and pumping blood through the body. It can usually be felt on the wrist or neck.

R

Reaction	When two materials do not mix, but change into a new material.
Reflect	When something is bounced off the surface of an object.
Reflection	A reflection can be an image seen in a mirror, or it can mean the action of light, sound or heat energy being reflected from a surface.
Reliability of data	The level of certainty it is possible to have about data.
Ribs/Ribcage	Bones that form a cage around the organs in the chest. They protect vital organs including the heart and lungs.
Rotating	Turning around an axis.

S

Sedimentary	A type of rock formed when plant and animal remains, sand, mud and stones are compressed.
Sexual reproduction	Reproduction requiring male cells (e.g. sperm or pollen) to fertilise a female cell (the egg) before a new animal or plant is made.
Skeleton	The structure of bones inside some animals.
Skull	The part of the skeleton which protects the brain.
Solid	A state of matter which maintains its shape.
Soluble	A material which will dissolve in a liquid, e.g. water.
Solution	When a material dissolves in liquid, the liquid becomes a solution, e.g. when salt dissolves in water the water becomes a salt solution.
Sperm	The male reproductive cell in animals.
Spine	The backbone; a part of the skeleton that protects the spinal cord.
Stamen	The male part of the flower.
Stars	Spheres of hot, burning gas that produce heat and light.
Stomach	An organ which is part of the digestive system that churns up food and mixes it with substances like acids and enzymes.
Sun	The star at the centre of our solar system.
Switch	A component for controlling the flow of electricity in a circuit, opening (off) or closing (on) a gap in the circuit.

T

Tendons	Bands of fibre which attach the muscles to the bones.
Thigh bone	The strong, thick bone in the upper leg which supports the upper body and helps the body to walk.
Translucent	A material that allows some light to pass through it.
Transparent	A material that allows all or most light to pass through it.

V

Vacuum	A completely empty space containing nothing at all – not even air.
Valves	Valves prevent liquids flowing in the wrong direction. The valves in the heart stop the blood from flowing backwards.
Variable	Something which can be changed or kept constant, and that can be measured during a scientific enquiry.
Variation	When living things, of the same kind/species, have different characteristics.
Veins	Blood vessels that transport deoxygenated blood around the body.
Ventricles	The lower chambers/cavities in the heart.
Vibrations	Produced when an object moves back and forth rapidly. Vibrations make sounds.
Vitamins	Nutrients found in foods, like fruits and vegetables, which help to keep the cells of the body healthy.
Volume	How loud or quiet a sound is.

W

Water resistance	A force created when an object moves through water. It acts in the opposite direction to the moving object and slows it down.

INDEX